ALSO BY ANDERS STEPHANSON

Kennan and the Art of Foreign Policy

MANIFEST DESTINY

Anders Stephanson

MANIFEST
DESTINY

*American Expansionism and
the Empire of Right*

Consulting Editor: Eric Foner

HILL AND WANG

A division of Farrar, Straus and Giroux / New York

Hill and Wang
A division of Farrar, Straus and Giroux
18 West 18th Street, New York 10011

Copyright © 1995 by Anders Stephanson

Printed in the United States of America
Published in 1995 by Hill and Wang
First paperback edition, 1996

The Library of Congress has cataloged the hardcover edition as follows:
Stephanson, Anders.
    Manifest destiny : American expansionism and the empire of right /
Anders Stephanson. — 1st ed.
        p.   cm.
    ISBN: 0-8090-6721-8
    Includes bibliographical references (p.) and index.
    1. United States—Territorial expansion.   I. Title.

E179.5.S82   1995
325´.32´0973—dc20

                                                    95-7623   CIP

Paperback ISBN-13: 978-0-8090-1584-9
Paperback ISBN-10: 0-8090-1584-6

Designed by Fritz Metsch

www.fsgbooks.com

40 39 38 37 36 35 34 33 32 31

To Anna

ACKNOWLEDGMENTS

I should like to thank Arthur Wang, Kevin Kenny, Richard Lufrano, Eric Foner, Richard Bushman, Betsy Blackmar, and David Armitage for comments and assistance. Because of the nature of this book, it is more than conventionally necessary to absolve them of any responsibility for its shortcomings.

CONTENTS

PROLOGUE

The 1840s were an expansive period in the United States, a moment when the right move at the right time could bring considerable rewards. By those standards, John O'Sullivan was a signal failure. His speculative business projects never flourished. His political friends in the Democratic Party never rewarded him properly for his publishing services. His conspiracies to annex Cuba failed miserably, almost landing him in prison. Though an opponent of slavery, he later supported the losing side in the Civil War because he also happened to support states' rights. His friend Nathaniel Hawthorne considered him bizarre, not to say a little crazy.

It is nevertheless to this same O'Sullivan that we owe the phrase "manifest destiny," which he coined in 1845 to signify the mission of the United States "to overspread the continent allotted by Providence for the free development of our yearly multiplying millions." Enormous expansion was indeed taking place across North America in the name of liberty, a liberty often also said to be "Anglo-Saxon" in spirit or race. From that angle, O'Sullivan's originating role is ironic, for he was descended from a long line of Irish adventurers and mercenaries. His political innovation earned him neither fame nor glory, nor even notoriety. He died in obscurity, with typically bad timing, in 1895, when the term, along with territorial expansionism, was about to experience a revival. His authorship was actually not established until 1927, chiefly because both words were bandied about very widely in the Jacksonian era. O'Sullivan himself was in fact unaware of having put together an expression until political opponents turned it into a symbol and an issue. So it became a catchword for the idea of a providentially or historically sanctioned right to continental expansionism. In that sense, it was anything but new. Already in 1616, an agent of colonization had ended a prospectus of fabulous green vistas in North America to an English audience with this rhetorical flourish: "What need wee then to feare, but to *goe up at once as a peculier people* marked and chosen by the *finger* of God to *possess* it?"

Here, however, I shall also be using "manifest destiny" in a wider sense, rather as Woodrow Wilson did when he wanted to accentuate the providentially assigned role of the United States to lead the world to new and better things. To him, what defined "America" was precisely this special calling or mission. The nation had been allowed to see the light and was bound to show the way for the historically retrograde. There was a duty to develop and spread to full potential under the blessings of the most perfect principles imaginable. This vision has been a constant throughout American history, but historically it has led to two quite different ways of being toward the outside world. The first was to unfold into an exemplary state *separate* from the corrupt and fallen world, letting others emulate it as best they can. The second, Wilson's position, was to push the world along by means of regenerative *intervention*. Separation, however, has been the more dominant of the two.

To imagine one's national self in this exemplary manner is not unique to the United States. Every nation-state lays some claim to uniqueness, and some nations or empires, historically, have even considered themselves on Higher Authority the anointed focal point of world or universal history. Yet, for example, the dynastic "Mandate" that legitimated Confucian China never envisaged a transcending "end" of history through a fundamental change of the world in accordance with its own self-image. "China" was an aristocratic notion of superior civilization. The Catholic Holy Roman Empire, a closer example, may have subscribed to heavenly transformation, but while awaiting the pre-destined end it was content to put the messianic vision in suspension in favor of institution-building. In the twentieth cen-tury, only one case compared to the United States in claims to prophecy, messianism, and historical transcendence: the Soviet Union. But the utopian impulse of the Soviet project is no longer with us. The American is, and vigorously so. A cursory glance at contemporary American politics is indeed enough to see the con-tinued presence of the ideological themes I try to map in this book.

My inquiry is thus about an apparent paradox: a particular (and particularly powerful) nationalism constituting itself not only as prophetic but also universal. Because this crystallized most clearly in moments of aggrandizement or interventionism, when there was a need to invest such acts with notions of essential American goodness, I have concentated on two periods of strong territorial expansionism: the 1840s, when the United States seized half the territory of Mexico; and the time around the turn of the present century, when war against Spain and the ensuing suppression of the Philippine independence movement added colonial posses-sions overseas. These studies, very much the "empirical" center of the book, are framed by two chapters of a more synthetic or reflective kind. The first attempts to delineate the origins of the American idea of providential and historical chosenness, origins both Protestant and liberal in nature. My final chapter, by con-trast, is an essay on how this idea has necessarily been trans-formed from Wilson to the present, a period when the United States, spasmodically and against its orientation, entered the fallen world to become its hegemon.

This, then, is a short book that aims to be both analytical and informative about a very large subject. The simplifications and lack of nuance that attach to such an endeavor are so obvious as not to require any elaborate apology. Nor is it the sort of work that demands extensive musings on theory and method. A few comments, however, are in order. It is primarily (but by no means exclusively) a study of ideology; synoptic accounts of social and political developments broaden the narrative and make the argu-ment more accessible to readers unfamiliar with the historical particulars. Nonetheless, the "original" part here is about national ideology, and in such projects there is always a tendency to lapse into culturalism of one kind or another, arguments that some ingrained tradition, culture, or ideal *caused* American expansionism. Manifest destiny did not "cause" President Polk to go to war against Mexico. No particular policy followed from this discourse as such: though certainly conducive to expansionism, it was not a strategic doctrine. Nor, I hasten to add, can it be seen as an American Idea or Spirit marching through history and "expressing" itself in various ways. In no way do I argue that manifest destiny exhausts or defines the "meaning of America," if such a thing can ever be subject to investigation. Other narratives can be told, about the popular attachment to autonomy, individualism, and the good material life, to mention but one. What I do argue, however, is that manifest destiny is of signal importance in the way the United States came to understand itself in the world and still does; and that this understanding has determinate effects. Manifest destiny, like all ideological power, worked in practical ways and was always institutionally embedded. Historically, it could become a force only in combination with other forces and in changing ways. Not a mere rationalization, it appeared in the guise of common sense.

I shall treat manifest destiny, then, as a tradition that created a sense of national place and direction in a variety of historical settings, as a concept of anticipation and movement. Both words have long lineages, which I have only limited space to pursue. "Destiny," the dominant of the two, can mean a whole range of things that are sometimes completely contradictory. It can signify, for example, necessity and chance alike. Here it will mean the idea of a prefixed trajectory of spatial and temporal aims for an anointed nation, though, as we shall see, the actual aims that are supposedly made "manifest" or revealed change in decisive and sometimes astonishing ways.

I have tried to avoid moralizing. Perhaps it had to happen the way it did.

MANIFEST DESTINY

I

CHOICE AND CHOSENNESS
1600–1820

British North America was colonized through conquest and subsequent implantation of replicas of British society, with the significant addition of black slavery. These colonies, on the whole, came to be functionally autonomous from Britain. Thus the system differed from the imperialism of the nineteenth and twentieth centuries, which typically featured a metropolitan center and a series of dependencies with subject populations. The North American model, however, had a strong pedigree, for "Europe" itself had largely been a product of it: Franco-German expansionism during the Middle Ages had created a fairly uniform Christian culture across a widening band of territory, bounded by a periphery of conquest and colonization.

In the early sixteenth century this normative community of Christian Europe was riven by the Protestant Reformation and the religious wars it induced. In the very same epoch, as it happened, the Americas were being "discovered"; and it was of course a particularly fierce and uncompromising phalanx within the Reformation—namely, the Puritans—that eventually colonized the region there known as New England. The name would soon take on a meaning beyond assertion of origins, for the idea of "England" itself already encapsulated a strong element of destinarianism. English Protestantism, early on, had developed a notion of England as not only spatially but also spiritually separate from the European continent, as the bastion of true religion and chief source of its expansion: a place divinely singled out for higher missions. The Separatists who crossed the Atlantic were part of this tradition, only more radical. Old England, in their eyes, had not broken in the end with the satanic ways of popery. Divine purposes would have to be worked out elsewhere, in some new and uncorrupted land.

Histories of the United States written after the Revolution tended to depict a straight line from this New England, indeed from that barren Plymouth Rock, to the full-blown federal nation in stride, thus asserting supreme title on behalf of the Separatists to the original spirit of "America." The success of this myth had something to do with the fact that historiography remained a New England preserve, at least until the advent of southern nationalism in the 1850s. Southerners had good reason to quarrel, for New England Puritanism had not been central to the development of the colonial world as a whole. Not even at the doctrinal level was Puritan domination complete. Southern Anglicans, for example, had played a leading role in the codification of slavery into American Protestantism. In Virginia, moreover, Anglicanism had espoused from the very beginning a deep belief in the notion of a Promised Land. Yet there was a crucial difference: Virginia was conceived as an *extension* of God's chosen England, not as a qualitative break or an Exodus from it. The New England Pilgrim Thomas Hooker could thus predict with confidence in 1631 that "the poor native Turks and Infidels shall have a more cool summer-parlor in hell than England."

Not everyone spoke with similar clarity, for the subject of separation, if not separateness, was fraught with political danger and philosophical difficulty. Yet New England was to be the most sustained case anywhere of a society molded in accordance with ascetic Protestantism. The Puritan break would then eventually serve to invest American nationality with a "symbology" of exceptionalism or separateness that has survived remarkably intact. In the Revolution, otherwise arguably one of the more secularized moments in American history, there was thus typically instinctual attachment to Puritan allegories and metaphors. When the imposing trio of John Adams, Benjamin Franklin, and Thomas Jefferson gathered in the summer of 1776 to select a national seal, each of the last two—deists at best—suggested images from the story of Exodus, while the Calvinistic Adams was, oddly enough, the one to propose a theme from classical antiquity. Jefferson also included a representation from the mythical Anglo-Saxon past he cherished so much as the putative source of the vigorous American sense of independence and liberty; but thirty years thereafter he was to return in his second inaugural address to his biblical theme of chosenness, evoking the providential hand that had led "our fathers, as Israel of old, from their native land and planted them in a country flowing with all the necessaries and comforts of life."

When "manifest destiny" was coined in the 1840s, apocalyptic Protestantism and utopian mobilization had actually reached a level unmatched since early colonial times. So it is no surprise that the expression should have been heavily suffused with religious overtones. Its origins, in fact, lay directly in the old biblical notions, recharged through the Reformation, of the predestined, redemptive role of God's chosen people in the Promised Land: providential destiny revealed. The world as God's "manifestation" and history as predetermined "destiny" had been ideological staples of the strongly providentialist period in England between 1620 and 1660, during which, of course, the initial migration to New England took place. Any genealogy, in short, must begin with the religious sources.

Yet it was more than an expression: it was a whole *matrix*, a manner of interpreting the time and space of "America." Seen from that angle, it belonged to the peculiar fusion of providential and republican ideology that took place after the Revolution, a most dynamic combination of sacred and secular concepts. Visions of the United States as a sacred space providentially selected for divine purposes found a counterpart in the secular idea of the new nation of liberty as a privileged "stage" (to use a popular metaphor of the time) for the exhibition of a new world order, a great "experiment" for the benefit of humankind as a whole. The Great Seal, in its final design, expressed perfectly this mixed ancestry of the religious and the classical: *Annuit coeptis; Novus ordo seclorum,* or, roughly rendered, "God has blessed this undertaking;

a new order for the ages." The motto had been lifted in bowd-
lerized form from the Roman poet Virgil, whose messianic
passages had always lent themselves to Christian appropriation.
Gracing our present dollar bills, the formulation would come to
epitomize the temper of the next two centuries more accurately
than was perhaps originally imagined.

What unified the sacred and the secular, then, was precisely the
idea of "America" as a unique mission and project in time and
space, a continuous *process*. The missionary aspect not only legitimated the enterprise but determined its whole meaning. My ensuing remarks will trace the religious as well as the classical-secular
lineages, with a view to uncovering how Americans came to understand their imperial extension and the particular peoples who
did not quite fit within this process of universal significance.

(2)

For Europeans, land not occupied by recognized members of
Christendom was theoretically land free to be taken. When practically possible, they did so. The Christian colonizers of the
Americas—including the Spanish and the Portuguese—understood theirs as sacred enterprises; but only the New England Puritans conceived the territory itself as sacred, or sacred to be. As
the appointed bearers of the true Christian mission, they made it
so by being there. To the same degree, England was thereby de-
sacralized. This, then, was the New Canaan, a land promised, to
be reconquered and reworked for the glory of God by His select
forces, the saving remnant in the wilderness.

The Puritan reenactment of the Exodus narrative revolved
around a powerful theology of chosenness that was to be decisive
for the course of colonization as well as for the later American
self-concept. A short (and necessarily crude) account of this theology is thus required. Some of it will strike the modern eye as
strange; but it must all be taken with the utmost seriousness, for
reasons that will be evident. I have singled out four salient
themes: (1) election and covenant; (2) choice and apostasy;
(3) prophecy, revelation, and the end of history; (4) territory, mission, and community.

Election and Covenant

Puritans inherited and reworked the Hebrew tradition of divine election as consecrated through the covenant with God. At a certain juncture, according to this tradition, God chooses the people of Israel to be His people in the fallen world: "Ye shall be unto me a kingdom of priests, and a holy nation" (Exodus 19:6). In turn, the Israelites accept, or "choose," Him. The sacred covenant, elaborated through Moses in the Exodus, is quite straightforward. If the chosen ones adhere to God and His law and, especially, do not turn away toward other deities, He will lead them to a predetermined spot of land, clear it of enemies, and allow His people a future of endless milk and honey. The initial focus is thus on a given territory (specified in a way not without effect today) and on the migration to it. The march through the wilderness to the promised destination is itself prophetic and revelatory, for it is a journey toward reconciliation with God. Hence the wilderness assumes decisive and sacred importance while the chosen ones happen to be there. But the territorial conquest, as it turns out, is not an end in itself. Through the New Israel, universal righteousness will return and the world will be regenerated. God and humankind will be reconciled at last.

Choice and Apostasy

The whole identity of Israel, then, is nothing other than this allegiance and mission, all according to divine plan. But the success of the enterprise is by no means predetermined, for it is based on a *deal*, and a deal can be broken, if not by God then certainly by His people. The Israelites might renege by choosing to do wrong, as indeed they do again and again and for which they are roundly punished. History is in that sense essentially a series of *choices* between right and wrong in relation to the contract. To that extent it is also a perpetual *test*. A massive responsibility is thus placed upon the chosen, for nothing less than the future of the world is in the balance. Anxiety, guilt, and relentless self-inspection are combined here productively with an ever-present imperative to intervene righteously in the world to transform it.

The American Puritans came to emphasize this perspective of covenantal chosenness, with some necessary changes in the historical particulars aside from the more obvious Christian differences. For them, too, history was a chronological series of covenants and choices on the way—spatially and temporally—to salvation and redemption. But over time there had been several moments of apostasy, irreparable breaches of contract as it were. The Jews, by refusing the Gospel, had failed to keep their part of the deal; the first Christians had flourished, but then degenerated and turned away too; regeneration had taken place through the Reformation; and in its wake the visible saints, the Puritans, had emerged as the truest of the true Christians, hence assuming teleological responsibility for righteousness and journeying alike in the exodus to the New Israel.

Prophecy, Revelation, and the End

A key part of that new responsibility was the task of rediscovering the True Word, buried as it had been under vast layers of interpretative falsification during centuries of popish heresy. To be a Protestant and especially a Puritan was to master the Bible as an epistemic code of revelation, to understand the always causally effective providential hand in the world. Current events were fulfillments or reenactments of the Scriptures. Failure to recognize this constituted atheism and apostasy. Every visible saint was consequently *obliged* to have an account of common and uncommon occurrences that was related directly to an interpretation of the Book. Hence there was a consuming interest in prophecy. By mastering prophecy one would be able to understand the course of history and "cooperate" with it. To be free was precisely to *understand this destiny* and conform to the direction of divine will, to "make our destiny our choice," as it was said at the time. Destiny, then, could be *known* because it was rational and predetermined, and because one was in possession of the key to understanding it. Once destiny was known with reasonable certainty, there remained the personal responsibility of choosing to follow it or to turn away.

No text was more prophetically important than the Book of Revelation, whose language would provide public discourse in the United States with allusions to an astonishing degree long after apocalyptic thinking itself had ceased to be central. Obscure but enormously suggestive, it offered the fullest vision of the end of history and the aftermath. It is a story of deadly struggle between the forces of good and evil, ending after many phases in final victory for the good and the Messiah's reappearance. What made the narrative especially compelling was the vision of the *millennium*. After a series of fierce struggles, the satanic forces are vanquished in the battle at Armageddon; Satan himself is imprisoned, and Christ rules together with the resurrected martyrs and the real Christians in peace and harmony for a thousand years. At the end of this millennium, however, Satan breaks loose and the truly final battle takes place, when the forces of evil are destroyed once and for all. Heaven descends to earth, proper judgment is meted out, and those not redeemed are sent to burn in Hell forever. The prospect of being on the wrong side of divine history was *terrifying* indeed. The millennium, then, was the last stage before the end. It was a period with all the marks of an "extended Sabbath," the metaphor often used in imagining the posthistorical utopia. John Milton, in England, described it more poetically as "Ages of endless date."

The Book of Revelation, in short, made sense to English Protestants in general and Puritans in particular. It allowed the Reformation to be interpreted as either a moment on the way to Armageddon or even as the Battle itself; in either case, it was a clear manifestation of an impending end. Surely, it could not have been an accident either that God had unveiled this New World, this new continent, hidden for so many ages, precisely at the moment when the process of purification had begun in the Old World. Even the mysterious chronologies in Revelation could be made, quite readily, to fit these monumental occurrences of recent times.

It is to the Book of Revelation that we owe the related concepts of the apocalypse ("unveiling" or "revelation" in Greek) and the millennium. They signal impending crisis and disaster, to be followed by a transcendental transformation of the corrupt earthly order into one of angelic tranquillity. The whole sequence is divinely engineered according to a predetermined plan. In this it goes beyond the merely prophetic, which accentuates the covenantal relation, the constant imperative of obedience, turning and returning to God and the law. The apocalypse is the ultimate crisis, externally imposed by divine intervention. Yet the very criticality of the moment renders human understanding essential so one can act rightly and not miss the opportunity for redemption. Divine omnipotence notwithstanding, apocalyptic expectation is thus a call for serried *intervention in the here and now.*

Territory, Mission, and Community

Early Christianity broke with Judaism in directing salvation at humankind as a whole: the divine vehicle was now the dispersed Christian community and so involved no particular spatial fixity. For historical reasons, however, *Respublica Christiana* became identical with Europe, indeed the very definition of it. Once territorialized, the geopolitical chasm between inside and outside became religiously charged and dangerous. Within, meanwhile, the Church was presumed to control divine destiny on earth, the utopian element safely confined to the monasteries. In destroying this institutional dualism of Catholicism, Protestantism reunited the secular and the sacred into a single worldly frame and thereby opened up the Christian potential for all sorts of utopian projects within it. Thus the Puritans, as we have seen, reinvented the Jewish notion of chosenness, migration, and redemption, the idea of a mission of spatial separation.

The millennium, consequently, could now be given a *location*, and it lay in the New World, the place for the end and ends of history, the place where one would do battle and reveal to the world what destiny Providence had in mind. Far from being just a simple outpost of European civilization, it was a sacred testing ground of nothing less than world-historical importance. Every activity, personal and communal, was irreducibly part of the holy war against Satan and the infidels. The aristocracy of saints had to work ceaselessly at this critical moment to make the present world as solemnly and gloriously Christian as it could be.

One result was to put great emphasis on the purity of the community, on always determining who was inside and outside, on eliminating deviance. Calvin himself had articulated the matter with typical bluntness: "It is the godly man's duty to abstain from all familiarity with the wicked, and not to enmesh himself with them in any voluntary relationship." The foundation here was the unquestionable rule of sacred law, at the center of which lay the covenant. A truly dichotomous view of sacred and profane thus combined with a pronounced *legalism* to shape a strong communal identity, a movement in constant advance toward the historical goal.

The message to the heathens outside was in this respect as radical as St. Paul's: see the light or perish in eternal damnation! Indians of New England thus faced the extremes of either submitting in obedience to God and His people or to an open-ended process of destruction. Temporary accommodation was possible, but *conceptually* there were no ethical limits to what might be done to them if they failed to comply. For the Puritan, the outside was profane, and the profane was that which had to be overcome, conquered, and destroyed, territory to be won. Any victory would then be a reassuring sign that Providence had in fact singled out New England for special dispensations. When smallpox devastated the surrounding Indian population in the 1630s, John Winthrop could thus class it as a divine favor. "God hath consumed the natives with a miraculous plagey," went the crisp verdict. (Benjamin Franklin would echo the sentiment in the eighteenth century, a less puritanical one, by lauding rum as "the appointed means" by which "the design of Providence to extirpate these savages" was fulfilled "in order to make room for the cultivators of the earth.")

This attitude toward the profane outside did not necessarily imply territorial expansion, for Puritans were unsure initially about the intended extent of the New Canaan and were inclined anyway to see the land beyond as "a hidious and desolate wilderness, full of wild beasts and wild men," indeed a sphere where

God had allowed the satanic enemy to roam about after the Fall. The outside, then, contrasted sharply with the sacred "wilderness" that was Puritan territory itself, to which the righteous had escaped from corruption in order to carry out God's will. For purposes of group cohesion, too, surveyable spaces were preferred. But as the theological thrust receded in urgency and economic development propelled the communities outward, it was not difficult to find expansionist justification in existing ideology.

(3)

After 1660, the decline in New England of the original sense of Puritan urgency generated clerical jeremiads about sinful ways and the need to repent so as to fulfill destiny; but when a regenerative outburst did take place through the popular Great Awakening in the 1730s and '40s, it was a highly individualizing and pietistic movement. Millenarian themes abounded, but their tenor had markedly changed. The fixation on cataclysmic events was replaced by a gradualist ideology of improvement, an emphasis on constructing the millennium by orderly progress, as it were. The apocalyptic seventeenth-century vision of the millennium became a millennium already in process, featuring individual agency in matters both spiritual and material but retaining the Church as a mediating institution. Jonathan Edwards, leading preacher and theologian of the Great Awakening, was central in this reconceptualization of the sacred-secular in the form of progressive time. Extending the idea of mission to the colonial whole of Anglophone "America," Edwards turned it into a place for ever-increasing abundance and fulfillment of the millenarian promise. Heaven and earth would become one, but over time; a "period of perfect peace" would then ensue in America and eventually the world as a whole.

An index of the change toward meliorism here was Edwards's ode to the "many contrivances and inventions" that were making life easier and allowing "more time for more noble exercise." Since God had already engineered the compass and so improved travel, it was only reasonable to expect more of the same sort. That America was now in the eighteenth century supplying the

world with material "treasures" was for Edwards a "forerunner of
what is approaching in spiritual things, when the world shall be
supplied with spiritual treasures from America." Convinced that
the new continent would begin "the most glorious renovation of
the world," he even speculated that the sun would begin to shine
from the west onto the rest of the world. Edwards was in fact a
theologian of the greatest philosophical sophistication and a severe critic of spiritual decline in America; but he is most important in our context for having enlarged the biblical frame to
include the advances of secular activity, and for having enlarged
the Puritan genealogy to include all white Americans in a protonational story, ready for appropriation by the nation to be.

Edwards died in 1759, well before that event. To the end he
remained a British colonial for whom French Quebec could still
be imagined as the Whore of Babylon, a typical term of oppro-
brium taken from Revelation that others would transfer a little
later to the "usurper" government in London. The clergy, however, were markedly quiet about the political events leading up to
the Revolution. Obversely, once conflict was under way, the clerical engagement became quite fervent. The Revolution made prophetic sense. The New World could be demarcated in sharper
ways from the Old, reconfirming that America was indeed the
fulfillment of the sacred promise, the beginning, perhaps, of the
end, another victory on the way to the millennial conclusion. English "tyranny," more directly, could be denounced in the familiar
terms of corruption and sin; and so in turn the political narrative
could be cast ever more firmly in the form of Exodus. Although
this religious interpretation was grafted onto the revolutionary
events and did not initially inform them, millenarian ideology was
widely disseminated through the clergy. Even Thomas Paine,
fiercely critical though he was of established religion, deployed its
language.

What were the advancements for which Edwards found so ingenious an accommodation? And what kind of society produced
them? Perhaps, after these theological considerations, a word
about social structure would not be amiss. The colonial world that
would presently rebel was in 1760 a series of regional settlements
along the Atlantic seaboard with various expanding "back coun-

try" regions. Its population and class structure differed significantly from the British, as did the political structure. Out of 2 million people, more than 400,000 were African slaves, largely confined to the South with its crucial plantation production of staples, such as tobacco, for the export market. The overwhelming majority of the white population was engaged in agriculture of one sort or another, including a vast class of small, autonomous farmers, *capitalist* farmers, who were producing food in growing measure for European markets. Thus British-style merchant oligarchies and landed gentry were dwarfed in comparison with the planters, slaves, and small farmers who had no real counterpart in the Old Country. In addition, large numbers of white males could vote in the colonial assembly elections. None of them were "outside" society, as were laborers and landless in Britain. There was also a crucial difference of religion. Three out of every four Americans in 1776 belonged to a non-Anglican, dissenting denomination, while only one in ten did in England.

Better off, relatively speaking, Americans were also a more mobile population. The desire to expropriate unused land (or what was categorized as unused land) for speculative purposes had already become rampant. A diverse, increasingly uncontrollable movement was afoot to stake out claims in the hinterland, claims for which one would demand clear and unequivocal title. Government, far from being an agency of communitarian development, was often reduced to the task of distributing and systematizing capitalist ownership in land. This would mark the post-revolutionary regime to an even greater degree. Then, with even the feeble colonial controls gone, additional territories and confiscated property opened up an enormous potential for new marketing of land. Rectangular grids, the sign of real estate, everywhere in the American landscape would be its most telling expression.

Culturally, the system was more homogeneous than we generally imagine, given the distances and varied origins of the white population. One reason, perhaps the central reason, was that American society was massively racialized, its identity overdetermined by the outward violence against Indians and internal oppression of blacks. Relatively open, equal, and thriving, the colonial world was also a society of white domination in the making; and on that note we may proceed to liberal republicanism.

(4)

The Declaration of Independence centered on a denunciation of tyrannical rule and an assertion of the natural right of free individuals to form a civil society. Toward the end there was also a covenantal nod to Divine Providence. The philosophical argument was most immediately inspired by John Locke. Historians of Revolutionary ideology, therefore, used to stress the influence of Locke's thought and the libertarian themes of his Scottish successors, such as David Hume. The emphasis, in other words, was on capitalism and liberal individualism. This view has been challenged in recent decades by a historical school that traces republican ideology instead to certain opponents of the corrupt court regime in England during the seventeenth and eighteenth centuries. In their attack, these English critics used ideas from classical antiquity, as reworked by Renaissance thinkers, about what made republics virtuous and stable. The argument, in its barest essentials, was that a political society built on citizenship could be successful only if the body politic exhibited virtue; since virtue was unstable and liable to be corrupted, so too was the state. Contemporary signs of "decline" such as factionalism, standing armies, patronage, paper money, and conspiratorial politics were thus decried as obvious subversions of virtue and personal liberties. By featuring a participating "social" citizen, this political orientation was not immediately compatible with crassly individualist forms of commercial "freedom."

If Jefferson's trajectory is any indication, the eighteenth-century colonials actually mixed these two strands of thought depending on the circumstances. From his Lockean Declaration of Independence, he reverted after the Revolution to a civic position based on neoclassical, Athenian conceptions of citizenship. Here he singled out the solid yeoman farmer as the appropriate social foundation for a virtuous United States. As cultivator of the earth, the farmer was dependent on no one and hence he was the archetypal American, essential in more ways than one. Urban life,

on the other hand, produced corruption and dependency. To secure the perpetuation of the yeoman class, Jefferson proposed a
plan of identically laid-out agrarian wards of ideal size; but these,
alas, were never implemented. He himself, of course, was anything but a yeoman farmer, being one of the largest landowners
in Virginia and so a sizable slave owner to boot.

The embodiment of that central American anomaly, this slave
master was also a quintessential exponent of standard Enlightenment ideas about rationality, human agency, and natural rights
for everyone. History, crudely speaking, was seen as the uneven
but progressive emancipation of the rational human subject from
superstition and irrational constraints, a process coming to an end
when this subject, invested by nature with certain rights, had become fully knowledgeable and everywhere supreme. Such a perspective was not necessarily incompatible with Christianity,
especially of the deistic variety: God, as the supreme incarnation
of rationality, had benevolently set history and nature into motion
and then retreated to watch His human subjects progress. At the
end, in any event, the liberated individual would be able rationally
to determine his own circumstances (women not yet counting as
truly rational) with minimal interference, yet also in accordance
with the "natural" dictates that scientific reason was gradually
uncovering. On that view, the historical meaning of the American
Revolution lay chiefly in allowing predestined liberty to break out
into the open, in *revealing* it. Being able to imagine "America" as
political revelation was clearly predicated on the fact that a good
deal of "liberty" along these lines was already extant in the land.
Put differently, the United States harbored from the very outset
an individualist and capitalist dynamic of considerable vibrancy.

It was also an *enormous* country; and territorial size was linked
directly to the problem of virtue through another classical prob-
lematic, that of republic and empire. The question, in short, was
whether vast territory could be compatible with a virtuous republic, in the American case one that was both new and unprecedented in kind. It was a pressing problem, for the American
confederation of 1783 ranked second only to Russia in size. The
Revolutionary founders, well-to-do and well educated too, knew
all the arguments. Rome offered the central reference point.

Since the Renaissance, it had been a favorite source of trans-historical "lessons" about the fate of states. On the strength of the Roman example, Montesquieu had demonstrated in the mid-eighteenth century that republics could not extend themselves by conquest and expect to reproduce their constitutional system, their true essence. Edward Gibbon's dictum a few decades later encapsulated the same imperial dilemma of Roman decline more starkly: "The causes of destruction multiplied with the extent of conquest." Altogether it was not a pleasant lesson to ponder for the Americans: internal degeneration of the republic into an imperial tyranny, concomitant militarism, and depravity. And there was an additional predicament, articulated by Machiavelli. If a republic was healthy to the degree that its citizens were virtuous (or "manly"), it contained, ipso facto, an inherent element of expansive, militant vigor; in which case there was a general tendency to corruption and eventual destruction. The defensive insularity of the Spartan model, in contrast, was not an attractive alternative, for it offered no vision of greatness and would expose the republic to security risks.

British opposition thinkers had circumvented this conundrum by conceiving a new kind of empire, an incorruptible empire of the sea, of commerce, of Protestantism, in short, everything that Catholic Spain was not. Extended empires of the *land* would inevitably set into motion the whole pattern of Roman corruption and decline; empires of the sea might escape it. Another neoclassical distinction, productive of a more favorable reading, was also available: that between empire as tyranny writ large and empire as extension of the rule of law over pristine wilderness. Thus one could comprehend *imperium* more soothingly as the enlargement of the *realm of law and civilization*. Empire would signify nothing more than a larger than "normal" territory.

James Madison, in a stroke of genius, famously solved the whole problem by inventing a wholly indigenous American model based on inversion. For republics of popular sovereignty, vastness was not a problem but a *blessing*, an insurance *against* corruption of virtue and decline. If embodied politically at the center in a series of institutional checks and balances, vastness itself would actually prevent any single interest, faction, or region from dominating and so destroying the whole. Coupled with Jefferson's imaginative system for contiguous reproduction of individual states, this federal solution laid the foundation for future expansion. After the 1820s, Jacksonians would indeed take the logic one step further and make it dynamic: popular republics positively *needed* to expand to stay healthy.

A second imperial theme, a commonplace on both sides of the Atlantic in the eighteenth century, is finally also relevant here: the idea of *translatio imperii*. It expressed, by this time, the agreeable double notion that civilization was always carried forward by a single dominant power or people and that historical succession was a matter of westward movement. One can see why this was an attractive idea. To the American eye, it gave historical sanction to becoming the next great embodiment of civilization. A series of "obvious" facts reinforced this view. The global circle had been completed: no more "hidden" continents to be discovered, nothing farther to the west, nothing now until the Far East, where the movement had originally started. There was a huge and empty land here to be transformed. The new nation was a condensation of all that was good in the hitherto most advanced and westward of civilizations, namely, the British. History could not conceivably evolve a better system of sustaining the liberty of man to permit the unfettered pursuit of his desires. Indeed, there could be nothing "higher," only more of the same. All this, then, was as clear as clear could be. "Westward the course of empire takes its way," Bishop Berkeley's celebrated eighteenth-century verse, would thus become the most tiresome of American clichés by the mid-nineteenth century, often in John Quincy Adams's modified version, which replaced "course" with "star." It was a marvelous substitution, for stars symbolized not only the expanding number of states in the Union but also *angels*, the providential messengers. Astral movement, constant and predictable, was a divine sign to be followed to the westward destination.

Strict millenarians had difficulties with the full version of *translatio imperii* because it connected America with the heathen past in a cumulative way, hence obliterating the sharp breaks and discontinuities. It made the United States the end of a potentially completely secular history. The polarity of the United States as a New Rome as opposed to New Israel would in fact produce quite diverging effects on foreign policy in the epoch of Theodore Roosevelt and Woodrow Wilson. Yet for now, in the post-revolutionary era, the *general* theme of westward movement was entirely in keeping with religious notions of a new and sacred beginning in a new and sacred land. "Empire, learning and religion," as the Reverend Thomas Brockaway preached in 1784, "have in past ages, been traveling from east to west, and this continent is their last western state. . . . Here then is God erecting a stage on which to exhibit the great things of his kingdom." What had originally been, for the clergy, a satanic space to be conquered was by now an alluring, pastoral emptiness to be exploited.

The Revolution, not surprisingly, gave rise to a veritable outburst of nationalist sentiment, of a sort, that in turn made possible discursive coherence around millenarian and republican concepts. George Washington's first inaugural address typified the mixture of biblical and classical language with its call for the preservation of "the sacred fire of liberty and the destiny of the republican model of government." Nothing illustrates the moment better, however, than the many poetic odes to the "rising glory" of America. The genre combined science and commerce, empire and millennium, into a final vision of "endless peace" under universal U.S. benevolence. A single sample will suffice to illustrate. It is from the pen of David Humphreys, Washington's protégé, officer in the Revolutionary Army, diplomat, execrable poet, and member of the Connecticut Wits, the first literary coterie in the United States:

> All former empires rose, the work of guilt,
> On conquest, blood, or usurpation built:
> But we, taught wisdom by their woes and crimes,
> Fraught with their lore, and born to better times;
> Our constitutions form'd on freedom's base,
> Which all the blessings of all lands embrace;
> Embrace humanity's extended cause,
> A world of our empire, for a world of our laws. . . .

Rhetoric of this kind expressed more than a pride in having managed to wrest independence from Britain, the most powerful state in the world. An immense new project, at once exhilarating and frightening, was under way. Everyone knew that. Underlying cultural affinities, too, certainly obtained throughout the ex-colonies. But as a *national* enterprise the post-revolutionary entity was far from clear. Contemporary France, the other case of "embracing humanity's extended cause," offers a telling contrast. Ferociously anticlerical in spirit, the French Revolution was also unequivocally French. It took place in a linguistically demarcated territory that had long been recognized, at least by the ruling classes, as "France"; it toppled a monarchical state with a strong domestic presence; and it was a Great Power with geopolitical enemies of long standing, enemies with which the new regime immediately became engaged in war. Making claims in the name of "universal man" was in these circumstances not meaningless but certainly fraught with limitations. Making claims in the name of the French people, on the other hand, was not difficult at all, especially not after the emergence of enormous citizen armies. None, or very little, of this applied to the United States, the revolutionary experience notwithstanding. There was no linguistic identity to claim, for it was shared with the British. There was no specific territory to claim, for it was growing and indeterminate in size and, besides, the status of the individual states and their relation toward each other remained unclear. Aside from the Puritan genealogy, there was no readily available mythology of ethnogenesis to which one could appeal. Nor, finally, did any post-revolutionary invasions mobilize, anneal, and solidify the citizenry in common resistance.

At the political level, then, this huge federation of states, with its potential for both growth and distintegration, had to confront the question of identity, what the national self might mean and how it might be projected. A set of simple symbols was required that would distill the past and at the same time proclaim the future. The extraordinary rapidity with which the Revolution was *monumentalized* actually showed the urgency: the revolutionary avant-garde turned into Founding Fathers, biblical patriarchs, Washington presiding as a near-deity, all evoked with ritual solemnity every July 4. In theory, there was otherwise nothing much one could put forth except subscription to the principles embodied in the Constitution, ultimately a purely *political* identity.

Imagining oneself as a world-historical community in process and a great experiment for the demonstration of higher purposes furnished the provisional resolution. The invaluable Puritan matrix could be projected onto more recent bourgeois models of enlightenment and profit, generating a modern nationhood of process and mission.

(5)

Humphreys became a Federalist in the 1790s, and indeed the world-redeeming impulse was at first chiefly to be found among some members of that political movement (though the brilliant and highly unorthodox Alexander Hamilton advocated power politics). The Jeffersonian ideal of a republican yeomanry, meanwhile, involved no imperative of world redemption, much less of course any Hamiltonianism. The United States, Jefferson insisted, was indeed "a chosen country," and the particular people Providence had chosen to fulfill the historic mission were the aforementioned farmers. No need for intercourse with the old and tainted world was thus envisioned—on the contrary, separation from it. In perusing the European past and present, what he found especially egregious was the crude and cynical game of power, "the exterminating havoc," as he called it. Considering the Napoleonic upheavals of that moment, he may have been justified. But between 1815 and 1914 it was not only the oceans and the absence of serious continental enemies that made possible the extensive geopolitical autonomy of the United States; it was also the British Navy and, arguably, the very European balance of power itself.

Jefferson himself actually had a keen eye for geopolitical logic, chiefly for purposes of continental expansion, which he strongly favored and greatly achieved. The "rising nation," he was pleased to note in 1805, was already "advancing rapidly to destinies beyond the reach of mortal eye." But contrasting the two worlds involved greater issues than perhaps he realized. These issues demand a brief exposition, for the Jeffersonian moment, with its dynamism and ideology of national aggrandizement, was to be emblematic of the nineteenth century.

The European state Jefferson abhorred was essentially an apparatus for war and the calculation of attendant dangers and benefits. The right to wage war for whatever reason one saw fit, short of completely obliterating the enemy as a state, was recognized as rational and legitimate: a nasty and brutish system, to be sure, but based on the idea that members in enmity were in some sense "equal." By the same token, there was no room for any universal ideology of moral right. Jeffersonians, on the other hand, could invest the American project with just such a quality of universal right; and they were able to imagine the United States as the embodiment of the interests of humankind as a whole precisely because their material conditions were so different. Their own state hardly merited the term, exhibiting none of the entrenched military esablishment and consequent tax apparatus typical of most European states. The external precondition for this happy circumstance was of course the relative security to which reference has already been made. Two internal factors, however, also played a role: the long British heritage of a "limited" state, in turn premised geopolitically on the dominance of naval power, which could never dominate state and civil society in the manner of large standing armies; and, second, the fact that untrammeled development of capitalist agriculture as such required no extensive state machinery. What it did come to require, however, was territorial expansion.

This expansion was implied conceptually in Jefferson's combination of agrarianism and radical anti-historicism. The past for him amounted to a sedimentation of irrational obstacles, preventing the struggling universal human being from freely pursuing his natural happiness. As the first people in freedom, Americans were now escaping this crushing nightmare of history and creating a completely new society. But in order to maintain this fortunate condition, every new generation must be given the material means to stake out its own future, provided it would always be an agrarian and pastoral one. Propitious conditions for agrarian recreation meant territorial expansion. Since the United States was the first space where man could really be free, such enlargement was by definition also a step in the liberation of universal man. It added to, in Jefferson's apposite term, the "empire for liberty."

Yet to define expansion in such a manner was also to declare any potential enemy *an objective obstruction* to the course of natural freedom, in effect to call for elimination and liquidation. A great deal of that would indeed follow. As Jefferson said with prophetic insight into the future empire, one must not tolerate any "blot or mixture on that surface." Initially, he eyed the whole continent, including even the Southern Hemisphere, from this angle, though he was unsure whether it would be a single federation or a collection of republics. But about libertarian expansion as such he had no doubt. After he assumed the presidency in 1801, his geopolitical vision proved as clear as his willingness to act.

There were four problems in extending the empire for liberty. There were the British in the north, controlling the St. Lawrence River and, because of the Napoleonic Wars, also causing problems for neutral shipping on the open seas. There were the Spanish possessions in the southeast and Mexico. There was the French rule over New Orleans and the territories west of the Mississippi. Finally, there were the Indians and the question of their "fate." Jefferson resolved the French problem with startling ease. Having approached the French with a view to buying New Orleans, he was offered the whole of Louisiana, an uncertainly delimited territory stretching all the way to the northwest Pacific. Against the prospect of acquiring national title to such a stupendous expanse, his constitutional qualms about presidential usurpation naturally paled. Thus he managed in a single stroke to double the size of the country for the presumed benefit of future generations of his citizen farmers. Henceforth, purchase would indeed become the preferred and morally correct American way of expansion. Even when adding territory through war, the United States would often insist on paying something.

With the French out of the way, one could turn to the troubled Spanish. Nothing, however, seemed to induce them to part with the Floridas. Only in 1819, when General Andrew Jackson had shown by undeclared warfare that the United States would eventually take them anyway, did Spain give up and sell. There was also strong American interest in acquiring Cuba, whose strategic position in the Gulf suddenly appeared vital to many. Madison, to no avail, had tried to buy the island in 1810. John Quincy Adams, who negotiated the 1819 treaty, thought American annexation of Cuba "indispensable to the continuance and integrity of Union itself" but destined to happen in any case because of the "laws of political as well as physical gravitation." Yet the United States decided to maintain a prudent distance. Any rash move against Spanish rule might turn Cuba into another Haiti, another nightmare of black insurrection in the name of the very same universalist principles that the United States presumably embodied, another independent black republic causing potentially catastrophic reverberations within the American South.

In the British case, finally, incipient conflict escalated into the vastly imprudent but limited and indecisive War of 1812, after which both sides became wary of confrontation and inclined to compromise. The cotton boom that imbricated the two economies in the coming decades would always serve as a brake on any too-adventurous moves, at least on the part of the British.

The three European problems had thus been resolved, mostly with great success. Security had been achieved and enormous territory added. "We are destined," as the retired Jefferson exclaimed in 1816, "to be a barrier against the returns of ignorance and barbarism. Old Europe will have to lean on our shoulders, and to hobble along by our side. . . . What a colossus shall we be, when the southern continent comes up to our mark!"

It was unclear if the fourth and final geopolitical problem was not actually an "interior" one. What was clear, on the other hand, was that the Indians were a sizable blot on the American surface. Little prudence and no compromise were necessary in dealing with them. By 1818, they had been eliminated as a serious military threat, defeated by future Presidents Jackson in the southeast and William Henry Harrison in the northwest. Estimates of their numbers vary, but in the territory recognized by the Treaty of Paris in 1783 as the United States, roughly the area between the Atlantic and the Mississippi, there had been more than 100,000 Indians, mainly in the south. A full half of the country, in point of fact, had then consisted of unceded Indian land. How that land was expropriated through trickery, legal manipulation, intimidation, deportation, concentration camps, and murder is well known. It is an instructive history of ethnic cleansing. My interest here, however, is in the ideological and legal legitimation, and what it says about conceptions of identity and destiny. In what manner could ethnic cleansing be inserted into the overarching narrative of destiny?

The Bible and natural law served as the two basic, partly overlapping authorities. Several biblical passages could be invoked. In Genesis, for example, God promises Isaac to make his descendants multiply "as the stars of heaven" and to give the countries of the earth to them; and Psalms has God offering His people "the heathen for the inheritance, and the uttermost parts of the earth for thy possession," in the course of which one is instructed to shatter the heathens "with a rod of iron" into "pieces like a potter's vessel." The fundamental message, as it was understood at any rate, was to possess, multiply, and fructify at the expense of the heathens.

A more precise elaboration of this was to be found in the natural law tradition. Here the essential aspect was the connection between possession and productivity, as condensed conceptually in the idea of *vacuum domicilium*. Emerich de Vattel, the eighteenth-century legal thinker, offered the standard reference (though Locke was also cited). On what grounds, Vattel had asked, can one "lawfully take possession of a part of a vast country, in which there are found none but erratic nations" which cannot "people the whole"? His response ran as follows. There was a given "obligation to cultivate the earth"—it was natural to improve nature—and these peoples manifestly could not do that: hence their title to the land was not true legal possession. The cramped Europeans, by contrast, could make real use of the land, *subdue* it; and thus they were justified in establishing full legal title.

In vulgar form, this argument boiled down to the dual proposition that Indians were hunters and gatherers and that the land was therefore empty, a "waste" there for the taking. Plentiful evidence showing that Indians were not in fact nomads was willfully ignored. And when it could not be ignored, other ways were found, as in the notorious case of the Cherokee nation. Constitutional rule, literacy, property, and other accoutrements of "civilization" among the Cherokees caused the white population in Georgia, as John C. Calhoun told an evidently sympathetic John

Quincy Adams in 1824, "great difficulty," the difficulty presumably being that of how legally to dispossess them. One solution, as it turned out, was to declare that by improving themselves and becoming stable agriculturists the Cherokees had broken existing treaties, and that, in any case, their essential nature was better served by removal to some suitably bucolic western setting. And removed indeed they were. Treaties with Indians, as the governor of Georgia unflinchingly put it, "were expedients by which ignorant, intractable, and savage people were induced without bloodshed to yield up what civilized peoples had a right to possess."

After abandoning his erstwhile notion that Indians would become dark-skinned versions of Enlightenment whites, Jefferson had in fact designated the Louisiana Purchase for resettlement purposes. This was at a moment when that vast space still appeared to be the "great American desert." When, in the 1840s and '50s, the reality was found otherwise, the tribal remnants were once again pushed aside. Americans wanted land to exploit, not indigenous peoples to assimilate. For Jefferson, at any rate, his original (1786) "certainty that not a foot of land will ever be taken from the Indians without their own consent" was duly replaced by the somber realization that government could not control white intrusion and expropriation, even had it so wished. Assimilation projects along Christian-humanitarian lines went on until the 1820s but generally failed. There remained expulsion or extermination.

The Cherokees, then, illustrated a continuing problem of defining who was to be included in the "real" America, socially and spatially. In 1831 the Supreme Court defined the Cherokees as a "domestic, dependent nation" and thereby allowed the categorization of Indians as subjects or wards—that is, as neither foreigners nor members-to-be of civil society. Other subjugated peoples such as the fifty thousand Creole French in Louisiana were first ruled as "children," in Jefferson's precise term, thus nullifying the supposedly universal right to consent to one's own government. The French were then swamped numerically by systematic immigration. All of which would offer legal precedent and experience at the turn of the next century when, as we shall see, new

alien subject populations would have to be classified as both inside and outside. Otherwise, American rule always replaced, culturally and legally, multicolored ranges with the stark, unequivocal
scheme of black and white: if not wholly white, then wholly black.
Shades and variations, *blots*, could not be recognized within the
empire for liberty. In the Jacksonian epoch, Senator Benjamin
Leigh of Virginia would express the spirit of either/or with ad-
mirable lucidity:

> It is peculiar to the character of this Anglo-Saxon race of men
> to which we belong, that it has never been contented to live
> in the same country with any other distinct race, upon terms
> of equality; it has, invariably, when placed in that situation,
> proceeded to exterminate or enslave the other race in some
> form or other, or, failing that, to abandon the country.

But no one was about to abandon this particular country.

II

DESTINIES AND DESTINATIONS

1820–1865

American nationalism emerged forcefully after 1820 but in the form of a diffuse disposition toward the world, for there was no clear outside to render its identity precise. It took the form of a structure of feeling shared by an "imagined community" rather than any explicit ideology. What one shared was a sense of an entirely new kind of country, uniquely marked by social, economic, and spatial *openness*. Common to all, too, was the related notion I outlined in my previous chapter, the notion that the United States was a sacred-secular *project*, a mission of world-historical significance in a designated continental setting of no determinate limits. This "nationalism," then, differed markedly from the European model which emerged simultaneously. For the latter emphasized permanency and continuity, a glorious past of a homogeneous nation in ancestral lands; and it supported the mythology by cultivating a whole corpus of putatively "ancient traditions."

The overall result in the United States, at any rate, was a dynamic capitalist orientation focused on westward expansion. The vigor of this development corresponded inversely to the feeble state apparatus, which had very limited reach. The federal role in the decisive processes of change was in fact nearly none. Armed removal of Indians aside, only the government's control of new territories and public lands much mattered; but this control was merely a temporary stage to prepare these lands for private ownership, to make them objects of cultivation and speculation. The imagined community, then, could roll across the expanse pretty much at will. The "nation," seen in that light, remained a series of temporary networks coalescing around endeavors of capitalist expropriation of space and subsequent development. Space itself, in a way, became the outside counterpoint for the projection of the national self.

Yet there was of course another side to this nationalism. I am referring to the emergence of sectionalism, the sign under which much antebellum history has been written since the aim is to explain why the period ends in civil war. It is indeed clear that subsiding geopolitical concerns and renewed waves of westward migration put into sharp relief the regional differences. Slavery, in particular, and the question of its limitation or extension threatened to undo the crucial balance between slave and nonslave states. The Missouri Compromise of 1820 postponed open conflict, but the problem festered ominously, always present when admission of new states (one every 2.5 years on the average) or annexation of territory appeared on the political agenda. Control over Congress here meant the potential power to make prohibition of slavery a condition for inclusion, or, alternatively, to establish that Congress did not in fact have any authority to do so. And behind that constant question hovered the more fundamental problem of already-existing slavery.

Opposing slavery did not mean that one was in favor of a free, multiracial citizenry living in republican harmony, though to their credit some radical abolitionists did so argue. Instead, one tended to be against *mixtures* as well as unfree labor. Loud calls for a "free" state often signaled an attempt to keep blacks out, coupled, at best, with some colonization scheme to rid oneself of blacks already present. But the issue had more than regional and moral implications. Cotton production not only was the engine of the southern economy but provided the country as a whole with vital exports at a moment when the United States was integrated into the world economy to a degree not reached again until our present epoch.

"Nationalism," in these circumstances, applied chiefly to the northern and western states. For it was here that one came to push the idea that these states were indeed united and entrusted with a sacred truth. A large contingent of New England historians, most of them clergymen, provided scholarly and popular justification for this notion in a period when interest in national history was burgeoning. And it was in New England, too, that Protestants began urgently to propose the American truth as a distinctly Protestant one, faced as they were from the 1830s onward with massive immigration of Irish and German Catholics. At the same time, an immense diffusion of religious movements was taking place amid the rapidly expanding settlements, forming a bewildering array of sects but generally putting forth much the same themes. By 1840, overall, there were forty thousand preachers abroad in the land, one for about every five hundred individuals, a proportion far higher than during the famous religious revivals of the eighteenth century.

The South, meanwhile, began to think of itself as a protonational grouping for which the real meaning of the Union was the liberty for individual states to carry on as they always had, a liberty conceived, quite logically, to include the right to secede. Symptomatically, the southern map exhibited few patriotic place-names. "Nation" there in fact turned by degrees into a code word for oppressive majoritarianism. Calhoun, revealingly, set out in the late 1840s to show that the term had been understood as the opposite of "federal" and deliberately excluded from the Constitution.

Conflict over nationhood, however, was not to come into the open in full force until midcentury. The predominant theme till then was actually not sectionalism but the individualizing ideology of Jacksonianism: opportunity and expansion for everyone amid minimal or no government regulation, a rhetoric of republican equality that actually masked a profoundly unequal society. Opposed to this Jacksonian-Democratic movement, if not to all its themes, were the Whigs, whose party managed to include conservative southern planters, northern merchants, and western politicians devoted to "internal improvement." Ideological differences between Democrats and Whigs centered on the role of government and control in the process of development.

If, then, the enormous fact of the Civil War is put into suspension for a moment, the struggle over "America" might be considered in terms of contesting strategies of development. Thus viewed, there were three distinct periods between 1815 and 1860, though none was ever homogeneous or noncontradictory. The first, lasting roughly until 1830, featured Enlightenment models of planning and organicist notions of community. The object was not spatial advancement for its own sake but orderly progress and balanced development within the territory already under control. Tradition and historical memory were salient ideas. Government, as the expression of popular sovereignty, was meant to serve a sizable role in creating the necessary infrastructure. The utter failure of the presidency of John Quincy Adams (1825–29) put a political end to this strategy, even if it survived in modified form within the Whig Party.

Next followed the period we are chiefly concerned with here, the Jacksonian era of minimal government, emphasizing the individual right to do whatever, and move wherever, one might please. Commonality, then, lay in the presumed equalization of opportunity. Freedom was an absolute and unchanging essence embodied once and for all in the Constitution. Any deviance from it in the form of governmental control was consequently corrupt and unpatriotic, usurpation to be quashed. Time, qualitatively speaking, had stopped, or ought to have stopped: no further "age" could be imagined. What remained was proliferating individual fulfillment of the original, sacred promise of freedom; and for that purpose there had to be *quantitative growth in space*, extension, in Jackson's own very fitting formulation, of "the area of freedom." During his presidency, sale of public lands was thus facilitated and accelerated; and the Indian presence, with the exception of the Florida Seminoles, was finally expunged from the southern map under federal auspices so as to make way for cotton. In the 1840s, Jackson's Tennessean follower James Polk implemented this logic on a much greater scale, adding, as we shall see, huge new areas to the empire of freedom.

In a dialectical twist, however, the territorial additions then served, because of the issue of slavery, to undermine the whole system by forcing the federal government to make fundamental *decisions*, something that it was, intentionally, never well equipped to do. These decisions pushed northern and western advocates of "free soil," territories where slavery would be prohibited, into seizing the political initiative. In the 1850s they recast Jacksonian discourse into a powerful argument against southern slave interests and thereby broke existing parties into pieces. Slavery was un-American, corrupting, monopolistic, usurping, and so forth. Government had to be restored to its properly neutral and facilitating role, while the aristocratic stain of the "slavocracy" was to be stamped out once and for all. The polarity had thus turned acutely antagonistic, and it took an altogether new kind of industrialized warfare to resolve it.

Where does manifest destiny fit in this? The great destinarian outburst occurred during the 1840s as a result of the need to understand and legitimate, or understand and oppose, aggressive annexation of territory. On balance, a considerable number of people did indeed oppose it, but to a striking degree in the name of the very same destinarianism as that of the expansionists. Southwestern annexation, for example, could be interpreted as the extension of profane slave power and hence as a sinful break with the God-given purposes of the land. An intense debate was thus unleashed *within* this discursive frame of American destiny. The nature of that frame, the kinds of claims that it allowed and disallowed, is the important aspect for me here, not the deeper and specific causes of expansion. Few of the arguments were new; but they were reinforced and turned into a more exact tradition, to be called upon when the moment so required.

After a short history of the central events of annexation—in chronological order Texas, Oregon, and Mexico—my analysis will focus on the destinarian aspects of the controversy they generated, leaving aside agitation that never went beyond being purely antislavery. The exposition will end with some remarks on the shifts of the 1850s that foreshadow the debates of the 1890s.

(2)

It is startling to learn from D. W. Meinig's great historical geography that in 1824 the United States of Mexico, as the former

Spanish colony then named itself, and the United States of America were not dissimilar in size and population: the southern nation spanning 1.7 million square miles with a bit more than 6 million people, the northern comprising 1.8 million square miles and 9.6 million people. By 1853, more than half of Mexico, a million square miles, more than the Louisiana Purchase, had been transferred to the United States. The discrepancy in population had increased exponentially, 23 million Americans compared to 7.5 or 8 million Mexicans. Geopolitical realities had, to understate the case, undergone a fundamental change.

Texas was the first province to be annexed. It had been created as a buffer area against the Americans when Mexico was still Spanish. Sparsely populated and distant from the Mexican heartlands, it became a tempting target for American cotton-driven penetration and land-speculation schemes in the late 1820s. The Mexican government decided to bring some order into a process it could not stop anyway by allowing American settlement under its sovereignty. Predictably, settler machinations soon began with the aim of renouncing that authority. The unstable Mexican regime decided to respond militarily in large part because the alternative of recognizing Texan independence would have exacerbated centrifugal tendencies in other, more important provinces. Though militarily inconclusive, the conflict led to Texan independence in 1836. The area was thereby opened for cotton production and the reintroduction of slavery, which Mexico had abolished in 1827. A rapid increase in population began. But when the Lone Star applied to enter the American Union, the answer was no. This was most unexpected. As early as 1825, the United States under President John Quincy Adams had tried to buy the province. But in 1837, Jackson's successor, Martin Van Buren, a northern Democrat, considered the moment inopportune. He was racked politically by a severe economic crisis; the annexation of Texas would have created one or even several slave states; and the operation was also fraught with unique constitutional difficulties, since Texas was technically an independent republic. Hence the negative response. The issue resurfaced, however, in the early 1840s in just the sectionalized form that Van Buren had feared. To complicate matters, the British were concurrently probing the possibility of aiding or protecting the new republic.

This was the situation when James K. Polk, following his party's platform, made Texas "reannexation" an issue in his presidential election campaign, claiming with little justification that Texas had been a part of the Louisiana Purchase and had been shamefully given up in 1819 by Adams (then Secretary of State) in the treaty with Spain. Polk defeated Henry Clay in the election by a very narrow margin and took this as an annexationist mandate of sorts. The measure was put through Congress by means of a simple majority vote and, after the slimmest possible victory in the Senate, Texas became a member of the Union. Thereby, too, the disputed Texas border with Mexico became an American problem.

The new President appeared to be a political hack. Adams thought he was "just qualified for an eminent County Court lawyer" and called him to his face, when Polk was Speaker of the House, "an Anglo-Saxon, slave-holding exterminator of Indians." Polk had been Jackson's drillmaster in the House, then served as governor of Tennessee but twice failed of reelection. It was not a distinguished record. He was not a man of nuance, and his political diaries reveal no sign of any analytical depth. But he knew what he wanted and accomplished it completely. One of the things he wanted most was territorial expansion, at which he was an astonishing success.

Understanding Polk's personal role in that process necessitates a comment about the historical place of foreign policy in government. International relations, as determined by the European state system, were conducted well into this century largely in "private." Chancelleries and foreign ministers managed their affairs in secret, at a remove even from the ruling elites and at times from their cabinets as well. Broadened rule and inclusion of lower orders in political society did not eliminate this privacy, except in open crises when multitude and establishment alike would suddenly get involved in a shallow sort of way. The American situation was peculiar insofar as the division of power gave Congress as a whole the authority to declare war and the Senate the right to ratify treaties, whereas the actual conduct of foreign affairs was left entirely to the Executive. Since expansion created geopolitical

problems with European powers and increasingly affected domestic politics as well, "foreign" issues were always latently present. In reality, however, as Jefferson's Louisiana Purchase showed,
the President had ample room in his executive capacity for ma-
neuver and manipulation. The trick, first and foremost, was to
present Congress and the public with a fait accompli. Polk was to
use this commanding power to push the country into war with
Mexico and nearly with Britain as well.

The two developments initially unfolded together. In his campaign, Polk had paired the "reannexation" claim to Texas with a
call for "reoccupation" of the whole Oregon territory, an equally
peculiar slogan since the United States had never occupied it in
the first place. Until the early 1840s, there were literally no more
than forty Americans in the entire territory, which covered everything on the Pacific between the forty-second parallel north of
San Francisco to Alaska. The area down to the Columbia River
was actually in control of the private Hudson Bay Company, Britain's imperial agent for western Canada. In 1818, Britain and the
United States had agreed to institute a policy of "joint occu-
pancy," or more accurately an open-door policy: neither would
have exclusive rights to the territory. In the early 1840s, the British
decided to press for settlement of all outstanding Canadian border
questions from east to west, and an initial treaty, removing un-
certainties to the Rocky Mountains, was concluded in 1842. The
remaining issues came up two years later but could not be resolved because of the American election. There were then more
Americans in the northwest, and demands were being made
within the Democratic Party for unilateral annexation of Oregon
in toto. Washington's actual position, however, had always been
to continue the border to the sea along the forty-ninth parallel.
Several factors, increasing migration apart, were conducive to
making an issue out of Oregon. The territory would be free from
slavery and so serve to pacify the North as regards the entry of
Texas. Similarly, as the area featured some of the few potential
ports on the Pacific, it was thought an alluring magnet for merchant and fishing interests in the northeast. American militancy
on the matter was partly a result of judging Britain, correctly, too
enmeshed in the cotton trade to be willing to put up much of a

fight, and partly a result of Anglophobia in election times. So Polk incautiously locked himself into a position of 54° 40' N (everything to Alaska) while secretly trying to settle for the forty-ninth parallel.

After war scares in the spring, such a compromise was eventually reached in June 1846. The United States gave up only what was dimly imagined as some barren, icy stretches to the north. Besides, it was widely believed that the British possessions, being in every respect so *similar*, would sooner or later become American anyway.

By coming to terms with Britain, Polk could intensify his moves against Mexico. His eye all along had been on the territory between Texas and the Pacific, especially Alta California (the present-day state of California) with the prized harbor of San Francisco Bay. The immediate issue concerned the disputed southwestern, formerly Texas, border with Mexico. Nothing essential was really at stake, but the dispute was useful to Polk in making the situation acute. Earlier, he had made clear to Mexico that a settlement should ideally also include the American purchase of San Francisco Bay with surroundings, possibly the huge New Mexico territory as well. A Mexican coup, however, had thwarted all hope for such an easy solution. There remained military action. Yet Polk and his advisers were not keen on any grand war effort. Senator Thomas Hart Benton's retrospective view was to the point: "They wanted a small war, just large enough to require a treaty of peace, and not large enough to make military reputations, dangerous for the presidency. Never were men at the head of a government less imbued with military spirit, or more addicted to intrigue."

The chief intrigue concerned the exiled Mexican general Santa Anna, whom Polk planned secretly to ferry back from exile and assist in resuming power, after which, in return, he would gratefully sell the desired territory to the United States. On the assumption that this would mean a short, little war, that indeed the United States would even be greeted as liberators, Polk confidently advanced American troops to the Rio Grande. When the Mexican army retaliated, Polk declared that the United States had been invaded and so war began. With an American army apparently already in battle, the Whig opposition chose to support funding for the war. Meanwhile, the navy and western irregular troops attacked California in accordance with long-standing secret orders.

Mexico lost the war in a crushing manner, but this had not been a foregone conclusion. The entire American army then consisted of 7,500 men, half of whom had participated in the original thrust into the disputed territory. With less luck it could have been a disaster. Of the 100,000 volunteers who eventually signed up to fight, 1,700 died in action, 11,000 of disease (the normal ratio). Compared to other wars, desertion was astonishingly high. The most spectacular example was the San Patricios, a contingent of several hundred Irish volunteers who actually switched sides. Among the casualties of the war were sons of Henry Clay and Daniel Webster, both of whom opposed it. Among those gaining military experience were Robert E. Lee and Ulysses S. Grant. The war effort had little impact on everyday life in the United States. There was no draft, the war itself was distant, and there was not much discussion of its actual prosecution, though dissatisfaction grew toward the end.

For, much to Polk's chagrin, the end dragged on. Santa Anna, having regained power with American support, tricked his foreign masters by rousing the country against them. Polk, throughout, believed that money was at the center of Mexican concerns and could not understand why there was no settlement. Yet the Mexicans refused to capitulate; and thus the Americans eventually had to seize Mexico City. A labyrinthic process of negotiation ultimately led to a treaty that was nearly rejected by Polk as too unfavorable. Within the cabinet and the country at large, a lively debate had taken place during the latter part of 1847 as to how much territory the United States ought to take, public opinion ranging from all of Mexico to merely San Francisco Bay. The first option was rejected for reasons we will explore below; the second for being altogether too modest. Polk himself wanted much of Baja California and a continental border much farther to the south than that specified in the final treaty. He finally went along because it was uncertain whether another Mexican government could be found that would renegotiate; and he dreaded the drawn-out guerrilla war that might ensue. So the United States acquired—after duly paying, of course—all land north of the Rio Grande and the thirty-second parallel to the Pacific. It included vast tracts controlled not by Mexico but by Apaches and other Indians. Also included were large numbers of Mexicans, all Catholics and thus presumed an indolent lot, people not about to be welcomed into the citizenry.

In 1853, the United States managed to purchase another strip of territory to secure routes for a future transcontinental railroad in the southwest. Four years later, President James Buchanan tried to buy much more extensive Mexican lands in Baja California and the northern provinces but failed. Continental expansion, *contiguous expansion*, had come to an end. Few thought so at the time. History and destiny, after all, seemed to suggest otherwise.

(3)

"In *America*," a foreign observer wrote from afar in 1848, "we have witnessed the conquest of Mexico and have rejoiced at it." The defeated nation hitherto had been "exclusively wrapped up in its own affairs, perpetually rent with civil wars, and completely hindered in its development." The best it could have hoped for in those circumstances was economic subjection to Britain. From a Mexican viewpoint, therefore, it was "an advance" now to be "forcibly drawn into the historical process" and "placed under the tutelage of the United States." Thus the opinion of Friedrich Engels.

Later in life, Engels would become more critical of such historical "advances." In this he was at one with his American contemporary Walt Whitman. The great poet, editor of the Democratic *Brooklyn Eagle* during the war, had found "miserable, inefficient Mexico" totally incompatible "with the great mission of peopling the New World with a noble race." I cite these two figures at the outset to indicate the political span of typical mid-nineteenth-century Western notions of progress. It is good to bear that range in mind when we now return to John O'Sullivan and the ideology of Jacksonian expansionism, which he expressed better than anyone else. Not only did O'Sullivan coin the phrase "manifest destiny," but his political sallies formed a veritable summa of the arguments of this type. His journal, the *Democratic Review*, is in fact more interesting as a source here than the widely disseminated "penny press," which echoed the same sentiments but evinced less of the revealing ambivalence and ambiguity.

O'Sullivan, after consulting Jackson and Van Buren, founded the *Review* in 1837 in order to give the Jacksonian movement intellectual and political presence in the domain of highbrow culture, which was then dominated by staid and conservative forces. Under his editorial guidance, the *Review* became the liveliest and most interesting journal of its kind. A whole constellation of future literary "greats" appeared in it. Hawthorne, a strong Democratic supporter, contributed from the start, but the new publication also opened its pages to Henry David Thoreau and Edgar Allan Poe, neither of whom was a Jacksonian. O'Sullivan mixed liberality of literary taste with a strongly polemical line, set by himself, in political affairs. It was the peculiar mixture of partisan politics and cultural openness that gave the journal its character. Though it never achieved great circulation, it was read by important people and became such a thorn in the side of conservatives that the *American Whig Review* was revamped in 1845 into a political counterpart.

Reduced to simple propositions, the views of O'Sullivan and his contemporaries now seem overblown and jejune. To maintain a sense for the rhetorical flavor (and of our historical distance from it), therefore, I shall make use of some extensive quotation.

O'Sullivan, as a good Jacksonian, spent the first years attacking the combined evils of consolidated government and banking aristocracy. Following Van Buren, he was also fully aware that he had "to stand aloof from the delicate and dangerous topic of Slavery and Abolition." In these early campaigns against what he typically called "delusive theories and fatal heresies," there was already a strongly destinarian conception of the United States:

The last order of civilization, which is the democratic, received its first permanent existence in this country. . . . A land separated from the influences of ancient arrangement, peculiar in its position, productions, and extent, wide enough to hold a numerous people, admitting, with facility, inter-communication and trade, vigorous and fresh from the hand of God, was requisite for the full and broad manifestation of the free spirit of the new-born democracy. Such a land was prepared in the solitudes of the Western hemisphere.

As "the nation of human progress," with Providence in support and "a clear conscience unsullied by the past," the United States was obviously unstoppable in its "onward march." Others had better take heed:

> The far-reaching, the boundless future will be the era of American greatness. In its magnificent domain of space and time, the nation of many nations is destined to manifest to mankind the excellence of divine principles; to establish on earth the noblest temple ever dedicated to the worship of the Most High—the Sacred and the True.
>
> For this blessed mission to the nations of the world, which are shut out from the life-giving light of truth, has America been chosen; and her high example shall smite unto death the tyranny of kings, hierarchs, and oligarchs, and carry the glad tidings of peace and good will where myriads now endure an existence scarcely more enviable than that of beasts of the field.

Democracy was in fact nothing "but Christianity in its earthly aspect—Christianity made effective among the political relations of men" by elimination of "the obstacles reared by artificial life." History was a providential plan whose end was to be played out in the specially designed space of America, where Jacksonianism had made manifest and transparent the universal truth of democracy. The cause of humanity was identical with that of the United States; and that cause was "destined to cease only when every man in the world should be finally and triumphantly redeemed." In short, Christianity, democracy, and Jacksonian America were essentially one and the same thing, the highest stage of history, God's plan incarnate.

This would seem to leave the Democrats with nothing much

to do except the administration of things and vigilant preservation of the sacred Origin. Yet O'Sullivan still saw need for battle against residual forces of corruption and enemies of truth. Culturally, there was also a tendency to ape European models, "bending the new to foreign idolatry, false tastes, false doctrines, false principles." However, as the very embodiment of historical truth, the people would see to the problem of false idols as well. His conclusion was indeed that the United States would not be led astray because it represented such a sharp break with the past. The "last order" in history was a completely new and completely *clean* civilization, free "from ancient arrangement" and so also free to choose destiny. "The scenes of antiquity" were of interest only as "lessons of avoidance." The future, and the future alone, was what mattered. (Herman Melville, after the Mexican War, put it more poetically: "The Past is a text-book of tyrants; the Future is the Bible of the Free.") The nation, then, was bound by nothing except its founding principles, the eternal and universal principles. It existed, as the "great nation of futurity," only in a perpetual present centered on projects and expectations.

Not much, however, was said about this "futurity," or about what the United States might actually do, other than being marvelous, to smite the tyrants of the world unto death. But gradually after Polk's ascendency over Van Buren in 1844, the idea of acquiring boundless expanses of land became prominent. For this land would preserve in neo-Jeffersonian fashion the original moment of freedom as perpetual genesis, struggle, and appropriation. Expansion would afford the swelling masses of the future, the "men of simple habits and strong hands," the opportunity of carving out a properly independent American existence, away from the claws of "the great monopoly paper-coining machine." This utopian impulse was unthinkingly coupled in O'Sullivan, as in so many other Jacksonians, with one speculative scheme after another, in his case wholly without success.

Jacksonian virtue, he firmly believed, translated into a pacific posture vis-à-vis foreign powers. Since people and government were constitutionally identical and the people only wanted "freedom to trade," American foreign policy would always be marked by "*peace* and *good-faith*." In keeping with this concept, the Re-

view followed an expansionist but pacific line, differing markedly from the many jingoistic elements within the party. War and blustering talk of national honor were inherently bad, peace and negotiation inherently good. The British, meanwhile, were singled out as particularly nasty exponents of the old anti-ethic of slaughter and conquest. In India and Afghanistan, they had engaged in "constant aggression, without any shadow of excuse or apology." Good thing, then, that the American system did not offer any "pretext or excuse for such wholesale oppression, robbery, and murder."

It is interesting to see this attitude come under pressure during the exciting but stressful sequence of Texas-Oregon-Mexico, which offered some evidence of both "pretexts" and "robbery," engineered by none other than a Jacksonian president. The least difficult question to face here was Oregon. As early as 1843 the *Review* took a maximalist stance, based on a critique of the "monopolistic" Hudson Bay Company. But when the issue heated up, the journal became a voice of moderation on the Democratic side, quietly suggesting extension along the forty-ninth parallel and carefully avoiding bellicose rhetoric. When one author indicated that war, while generally a bad thing, would finally liberate Americans from their cultural "thraldom" to Britain and cleanse "the political atmosphere," he was rebuked in an editorial note that declared war "an unmixed evil in its moral influences" that could never have any "benefits on the national spirit and character." War with the British, cads though they were, would ultimately be a great calamity.

In his short-lived popular paper the *Morning Star*, however, O'Sullivan maintained the original maximalism, while not calling for war. It was in this context that, on December 27, 1845, he proclaimed

> the right of *our manifest destiny* to overspread and to possess the whole continent which providence has given us for the development of the great experiment of liberty and federated self government. [Italics added]

Congress, at the time, was debating Oregon, and a member of the Whig opposition, in the course of denouncing the idea of "a universal Yankee nation," picked up the expression for ridicule, thus inadvertently helping to make it a staple of the political language of American history. But O'Sullivan and others had deployed the two words constantly. He had in fact used the expression six months earlier with regard to Texas annexation without any special notice.

The Oregon issue had barely been settled before the *Review*, in a sudden change of tone, published a lyrical ode to the coming fusion of England's manufacturing and American agriculture through the mechanism of free trade. The occasion was the repeal of the restrictive British corn laws and the commercial visions of American exports that this induced: "the Anglo-Saxon race" would be reunited (under American dominance) and prosperity ensue for all. The new economic theme articulated an underlying fact: powerful Britain, land of the Anglo-Saxons, was not Mexico. The two could not be conceived in the same frame.

A kind of geographical determinism originally governed O'Sullivan's views on Texas. Anyone, he said in April 1844, who "cast a glance over the map of North America" would see that Texas was "a huge fragment, artificially broken off" from its proper continental setting, a setting "symmetrically planned and adapted in its grand destiny" and duly "in the possession of the race sent there for the providential purpose." An impartial observer, therefore, would have to conclude that Texas "*must*, sooner or later, come together into one homogeneous unity" with the rest. Reading maps and spatial configurations in such a manner was common in the educated Western world of the nineteenth century. From a religious viewpoint, it was obvious that God had laid out the landscape with some intention in mind. From a rationalist perspective it was obvious that nature was not an accidental heap of materials but a system whose inner logic could be uncovered by scientific analysis. The two perspectives generally could indeed be reconciled in "natural theology": the real was rational and thus subject to inherent, natural laws, which in turn had been divinely engineered. In the United States, geographical rationalism had a most reputable pedigree. Jefferson had considered New Orleans a "natural" (hence rightful) possession of the United States, and his comprehension of the Floridas followed the same pattern. Henceforth, cartographically minded politicians would find various "natural borders" to invoke, depending on the historical moment: the St. Lawrence River, the Mississippi, the Rocky Mountains, Hudson Bay, the Gulf of Mexico, the Pacific, the North American continent, even the Sandwich Islands (Hawaii). By the 1850s, it was in fact possible to think of the Caribbean islands as "naturally" American on account of their being the natural, effluvial result of the Mississippi.

Having read his map, O'Sullivan was less sure how to make the natural occur in real life. He was still wedded to the principle of morally impeccable expansion and insisted, therefore, that Mexico must agree before Texas annexation could take place. Such a "poor neighbour" ought not to be bullied. But by early 1845, after his political switch to Polk, he was favoring immediate annexation, now finding the neighborly complaints "the most insolent farce ever attempted even by the bombastic absurdity of Mexican conceit and imbecility." Worse still was the "traitorous Anti-Americanism" at home that was attempting to depict annexation by "misrepresentation and sophism" as "an act of national rapacity, spoliation, and bad faith," whereas in fact the behavior of "our great, pacific and friendly Union" had been extraordinarily restrained. It was with great satisfaction, therefore, that he took note in mid-1845 of the congressional assent to annexation:

Texas has been absorbed into the Union in the inevitable fulfillment of the general law which is rolling our population westward. . . . It was disintegrated from Mexico in the natural course of events, by a process perfectly legitimate on its own part, blameless on ours; and in which all the censures due to wrong, perfidy and folly, rest on Mexico alone.

He went on to predict that California would be the next candidate for annexation: "Already the advance guard of the irresistible army of Anglo-Saxon emigration has begun to pour down upon it, armed with the plough and the rifle, and marking its trail with schools and colleges, courts and representative halls, mills and meeting-houses." The reality was less idyllic. In 1848, when California did become American territory, the condition of its Hispanic population deteriorated markedly; and when "the irre-

sistible army of Anglo-Saxon emigration" came marching in to
pursue land, gold, and profits, it was as usual a genocidal catas-
trophe for the Indian population.

Once Texas had been secured, O'Sullivan was remarkably quick
in speculating on the virtues of gobbling up all of Mexico, laying
out before the war the parameters of what would turn into a
heated debate only in late 1847. He assumed that the southern
neighbor would "become an integral portion of these United
States at some future period" but thought it not a good idea for
the moment because "the entire Mexican vote would be substan-
tially below our national average both in purity and intelligence."
Inclusion might also give rise to consolidated rule from the federal
center, always something to be dreaded. Still, the march was on
and so an obvious dilemma had arisen: "Democracies must make
their conquests by moral agencies. If these are not sufficient, the
conquest is robbery." His solution was pacific penetration by *commercial means*, which would "beget a community of interest between us" while suitably instilling in the Mexicans "confidence
and respect for our institutions." Americans would gain an outlet
for their right to pursue their interests and Mexicans would learn
the ways of the future in good time. Through the "moral" education emanating from commerce, then, "the whole of this vast
continent is destined one day to subscribe to the Constitution of
the United States," whereas "a sword drawn to hasten the event"
would detract from its value.

He wrote this to stem a flood of enthusiastic annexationism
within his own party in the wake of the Texas victory. There was
already a danger, as he saw it, that the United States would "be
obliged, in self-defense, to assume an aggressive attitude towards
Mexico," in which case it would be exceedingly difficult to avoid
"an end short of absolute subjugation." And on that note the
matter rested. The *Review* remained conspicuously low-key when
war actually did break out. Nothing substantial was in fact said
on the subject of Mexico between October 1845 and February
1847. A certain unease about Polk's war was probably one reason;
another, more prosaic, was that O'Sullivan sold the journal in
1846, and though he continued to write editorials now and then,
the polemics about foreign affairs declined in frequency. He him-

self commenced a private campaign to persuade the administration to buy Cuba. Polk was won over to the idea, but the ensuing
proposal to the Spanish government was rebuffed in no uncertain
terms. O'Sullivan then shifted his focus to conquering the island
by conspiring with Cuban interests in the United States, but the
ensuing expeditions failed and almost got him convicted of breaking American neutrality laws.

Apprehensions about the legitimacy of the war against Mexico
were gone, in any event, when the *Review* resumed serious cov-
erage in 1847. Racial inflections now marked the tone, and the
narrative was framed around how constant had been the historical
advance of the American "race of hardy pioneers." Thus "barbarism" and "the savages" were said to have given way naturally
to "the intelligent and peaceful settler," a process that differed
fundamentally and favorably from European models of military
invasion. While Americans had shown "democratic energy and
enterprise" in "driving back the Indians, or annihilating them as
a race," the Spanish conquerors of Mexico had showed no such
spirit of mission. But if Christianization, civilization, and cultivation of the land had been sadly lagging, change was now in the
works because of "the descent of the northern race." Yet because
"the degraded Mexican-Spanish" were in no state to receive the
"virtues of the Anglo-Saxon race," there could be no talk of any
"political union." That same degradation, however, also made
peaceful "accommodation" impossible: the opponent was simply
incapable of acting reasonably. The only feasible result of the war,
therefore, was "the annihilation" of Mexico "as a nation." Americans were obliged to seize control of the country and "settle its
affairs." What O'Sullivan had feared in 1845 had seemingly come
to pass.

Yet the Mexican vanishing act, however the *Review* imagined
it, could not occur in the near future for there were millions of
them; and while one might envisage a time when "every acre of
the North American continent" would be peopled "by citizens of
the United States," the task of settling the affairs of Mexico was,
on balance, fraught with danger to the true spirit of America. A
drawn-out effort would stimulate domestic militarism and so create vested interests dominated by the Whigs. Better, then, to take
California and New Mexico against proper payment and let time

take care of the rest. Nothing, at any rate, was more important than keeping the millions of "proverbially indolent" out of the American "political family."

Thus the prospect of dilution of American purity caused the *Review* to shrink before the actual task of extensive rearrangement of Mexico's affairs. Earlier, O'Sullivan had in fact singled out "homogeneity" as *the* factor that would make the American empire a lasting one. Its territory would be enormous, but similarity of "laws and institutions" would nevertheless make it "compact"; and the people themselves would also "be homogeneous." Other empires, past and present, had fallen precisely because of their "dissimilar and hostile materials." Hence, while "England must fade" and "the colossus of Russia must crumble," the empire of freedom would remain.

And so, one is bound to say, it has happened. The United States would have to go through a wrenching civil war to achieve unity, and the ensuing American empire would eventually be anything but homogeneous in population. But it has lasted in no small measure because of its insistence on constitutional homogeneity, its refusal of any room for territorialized differences of any significance within its continental compass. The precondition of that success, on the other hand, lay in the contradictory process, expressed with unconscious irony above, of peaceable settlers engaged in lofty acts of annihilation. Peace and annihilation were seemingly two sides of the same coin. Meanwhile, the other two empires are now in fact gone, a century or so later than O'Sullivan probably expected but partly for the very reasons he indicated: heterogeneity and "hostile materials." His early notion, it should be added, of elevating Mexico to American standards through the blessings of free trade, achieving the manifest destiny through economic flows, has a certain late-twentieth-century ring to it.

It may be suitable, in view of the general content of the *Review*, to end this exposition in a literary vein with a sonnet by William Gilmore Simms, a leading southern intellectual. His poem appeared in early 1846 under the title "Progress in America":

The adventurous Spaniard crack'd th' Atlantic's shell—
   Though not for him to penetrate the core.
The good old Norman stock will do as well,

Nay, better; a selected stock of old
    With blood well-temper'd, resolute and bold;
Set for a mighty work, the way to pave
    For the wrong'd nations, and, in one great fold,
Unite them, from old tyrannies to save!
We do but follow out our destiny,
    As did the ancient Israelite—and strive,
Unconscious that we work at His decree,
    By Whom alone we triumph as we live!

These heroic commonplaces of American chosenness expressed
a spirit that was least of all "unconscious," as the poet paradoxi-
cally argued. Seldom has there been a more articulated, explicit
awareness of working His decrees in every way.

On that note we may turn to the critiques, or *partial* critiques,
of territorial expansionism, often formulated in terms every bit as
destinarian as those of the most extreme expansionists.

(4)

It is useful first to get a rough idea of the fault lines of political
opinion in the country at large. Northwestern and mid-Atlantic
Democrats were most consistently in favor of expansion and destinarian language; and the opposition, as one would expect,
largely followed party and sectional lines as well. Northern Whigs
tended to be against unruly continentalism, though very few said
no in the end to harbors on the Pacific coast. They disliked extension generally because it threatened to create an uncontrollable land mass without community and organic ties. However,
while denouncing Texas annexation and the war, they voted to
fund the latter. Southern Whigs favored acquisition of Texas but
still liked Jefferson's old idea of new, independent republics based
on American principles. Once Texas had been brought in, some
southeastern Democrats, preeminently Calhoun, became bitterly
opposed to any more conquest. On racial grounds, chiefly, they
were against taking all of "mongrel" Mexico, where the prospects
for slavery were in any event bad. Southerners also opposed any
annexation that prohibited slavery a priori, as the famous Wilmot

Proviso, introduced by a northern Democrat in 1846, proposed to do. Proviso Democrats liked territorial aggrandizement but wanted it to be free, which also meant essentially *white*. Ultimately, the most vociferous criticism of annexationism came from Protestant groups in New England which took for granted that Texas entry and the war were conspiracies of the "slavocracy." It is within this camp that one finds the clearest critiques of expansionism. Churches and evangelicals otherwise reflected sectional divisions, but not entirely; some northerners saw expansion against a Catholic power as expansion for Christ. "Public" sentiment as a whole is hard to evaluate, but it seems to have been commonly, if diffusely, supportive of enlargement. Why not?

To determine the discursive extent to which one could indeed say no, I will look more closely at the New England clerics and intellectuals, since this was a period when such individuals mattered. The traditional northern Whig opposition and the Proviso supporters will also come under scrutiny. Because of his early historic role in continental expansionism and equally historic role in abolitionism later on, John Quincy Adams will be the object of some brief remarks. The section ends with a brief exposition of the views of Adams's innovative follower William Seward and his ideas of a commercial empire.

In some ways, the most illuminating critique of manifest destiny appeared eight years before the expression appeared in print. In 1837, when Texas annexation was first on the agenda, William Ellery Channing, founder of the Unitarian Church in the United States and a prominent Boston preacher, wrote an open letter to Henry Clay. This tract of some 20,000 words was widely disseminated and played a considerable role in preventing annexation at that moment. Channing offered a scathing historical review of the Anglo-Texan insurrection against Mexico, the perpetrators of which had had the scandalous temerity to evoke the example of the American Revolution when their action had really been a criminal attempt to sanction the spread of slavery and "the mighty frauds" of land speculation. Condensed to its basic point, his eloquent epistle was an exhortation to the American people not to choose the wrong way. History showed that Providence meant to elevate everyone, especially the laboring and the downtrodden, to a civilized Christian life of respect, tolerance, and free-dom. No country had been more blessed in this regard, despite the monstrous evil of slavery, than the United States. Here, then, there ought to be no grounds for any temptation and apostasy. To give in to expansionism, rapacity, and greed, to choose wrong, was therefore doubly disgraceful: a sin in itself, and a particular sin for this nation, an enormously privileged one facing no hostile foreign powers and no material deprivation. Such a nation, on the contrary, ought to provide its less fortunate "sister republics" with support, assume the role of a "sublime moral empire" with a mis-sion "to diffuse freedom by manifesting its fruits," not to plunder, "crush and destroy." Yet, as Channing darkly remarked, American culture was already showing signs of having chosen deviation. Freedom was being used as a means for insatiable gain and not for ennobling purposes. Choosing criminality in the Texas case might then well hurl the country off the straight and narrow forever.

In the course of his letter to Clay, Channing took a solid swipe at destinarian justifications:

It is sometimes said, that nations are swayed by laws, as un-failing as those which govern matter; that they have their destinies; that their character and position carry them for-ward irresistibly to their goal . . . that, by a like necessity, the Indians have melted before the white man, and the mixed, degraded race of Mexico must melt before the Anglo-Saxon. Away with this vile sophistry! There is no necessity for crime. There is no Fate to justify rapacious nations, any more than to justify gamblers and robbers, in plunder. We boast of the progress of society, and this progress consists in the substitutions of reason and moral principle for the sway of brute force. It is true, that the more civilized must always exert a great power over less civilized communities in their neighbourhood. But it may and should be a power to en-lighten and improve. . . . We are *destined* (that is the word) to overspread North America; and, intoxicated with the idea, it matters little to us how we accomplish our fate. To spread, to supplant others, to cover a boundless space, this seems our ambition, no matter what influence we spread with us. Why cannot we rise to noble conceptions of our destiny?

Channing's forceful intervention was in part biblical prophecy. Like God's erstwhile chosen people, the Israelites, Americans are always in the process of making the moral choice of turning toward God's universal love or away from it. In case of the latter, the sinful nation is certain to incur proper providential punishment, not perhaps through miraculous devastation but by the overwhelming growth of corruption and subversion within, thus rendering the original promise null and void. But exhortation aside, what gave Channing's argument its singular power was in no small measure the historical demonstration that most of the claims made in the name of Texan emancipation were hypocritical humbug. The final court of appeal, though, as he himself stated unapologetically, was *moral and religious values*, a voluntarist call to regeneration. The United States had been assigned a purpose in the unfolding of the providential plot that was being perverted. Hence the call for repentance and, in a key phrase, "self-restraint," the language of self-mastery, the imperative of repressing temptation and desire.

Channing died in 1842, well before perversion finally set in. A year later his nephew, William Henry Channing, preacher, editor, and deeply influenced by utopian socialism, wrote in the same spirit of "the sublime destinies of this Christened though not Christianised Anglo-Saxon Race" that had broken the providential "trust" by "savage robberies of the Indians" and "cruel and wanton oppressions of the Africans." When war came, he condemned it in no uncertain terms. Among other things, it would "divert our whole people from the fulfillment of the destiny to which Providence plainly summons us." Yet some of his fellow "Associationists" within the utopian Brook Farm movement revealed the more common, fatalistic terminus of the radical line of argument:

There can be no doubt of the design being entertained by the leaders and instigators of this infamous business, to extend the "area of freedom" to the shores of California, by

robbing Mexico of another large mass of her territory; and
the people are prepared to execute it to the letter. In many
and most aspects in which this plundering aggression is to be
viewed it is monstrously iniquitous, but *after all* it seems to
be completing a more universal design of Providence, of extending the power and intelligence of advanced civilized
nations over the whole face of the earth, by penetrating into
those regions which seem fated to immobility and breaking
down the barriers to the future progress of knowledge of the
sciences and arts: and *arms seem to be the only means by
which this great subversive movement towards unity among
nations can be accomplished.* . . . In this way Providence is
operating on a grand scale to accomplish its designs, making
use of instrumentalities ignorant of its purposes, and incited
to act by motives the very antipodes of those which the real
end in view might be supposed to be connected with or grow
out of. [Italics added]

Fatalistic resignation before a long-term providential design
marked one obvious way of closing the contradiction that Channing had opened up: horrible things are happening for horrible
reasons, but this is not as bad as it looks because through these
means Providence has chosen, as far as one can tell from history,
to lay the foundations for a future unification of humankind into
one harmonious, scientific whole. Criminality had thus become
acceptable as destiny and history.

Harmonious unification along global lines was a leading theme
in the kind of Christian socialism embraced by Brook Farm in its
brief career as one of the most important of the myriad reform
movements of the 1840s; but the strategy by which perversion of
national purpose as a question was recoded into providential historical design was common to a whole host of intellectuals, most
of whom had been influenced, directly or indirectly, by German
and English romanticism. The matter was not merely academic.
Consider the example of George Bancroft, the first great American historian. He was unusual among New England intellectuals
in being a card-carrying Democrat and because he had been educated at German universities. National-romantic sensibilities

were not a German invention, but they received their most advanced articulation there; and Bancroft's subsequent multivolume history of the United States would be thoroughly informed by it. But so too would his work as Polk's Secretary of the Navy, in which capacity he planned the attack on California. For Bancroft the American Revolution "promised the regeneration of the world"; and to him Andrew Jackson represented the kind of world-historical figure that Napoleon had been for Hegel.

Ralph Waldo Emerson, the preeminent New England intellectual, had no such immediate connection to the affairs of state, but his appropriation (through British sources) of German romanticism into a homespun, unorthodox kind of providentialism carried enormous weight in that flourishing cultural moment of the 1840s and '50s sometimes referred to as the American Renaissance. Emerson, in his maddeningly indirect way, said diverging things about "America" but generally held it to be "a last effort of the Divine Providence in behalf of the human race," a radical "beginning of a new and more advanced order of civilization," or, more poetically, "the home of man" which would stretch "to the waves of the Pacific sea." Belief in "a sublime and friendly Destiny," the fundamental nature of which was apparently "that love and good are inevitable, and in the course of things," made it easier for Emerson to swallow the annexation of Texas despite slavery. It may appear, he said, "one of those events which retard or retrograde the civilization of ages," but in the end "the World Spirit is a good swimmer, and storms and waves cannot easily drown him." He opposed the Mexican War but did nothing much to resist it. He remained, in the end, mired in fatalistic passivity: "It is very certain that the strong British race, which has now overrun so much of this continent, must also overrun that tract [Texas], and Mexico and Oregon also, and it will in the course of the ages be of small import by what particular occasions and methods it was done. It is a secular question."

Indeed, the philosophical and literary community of the North dithered a great deal on the political developments of the 1840s, antislavery notwithstanding; and this was a community that mattered politically at the time. Destinarian thinking abounded. Emerson's friend and collaborator Theodore Parker is an inter-

esting case because, together with Bancroft, he was the most politically minded of the lot (and as a clergyman also a typically
organic, a socially embedded, intellectual of New England). The
Mexican War he found "mean and wicked" and quite the wrong
way to go about things. Before long, it was true, the United States
would "possess the whole of the continent":

> But this may be had fairly; with no injustice to any one; by
> the steady advance of a superior race, with superior ideas and
> a better civilization; by commerce, trade, arts; by being better
> than Mexico, wiser, humaner, more free and manly.

About the direction of history, then, Parker had little doubt. It
was evident that the "history of the Anglo-Saxon, for the last
three hundred years, has been one of continual aggression, invasion, and extermination"; and consequently, it was evident, too,
that "God often makes the folly and the sin of men contribute
to the progress of mankind." Yet civilization had progressed far
enough to put war, inherently always a crime in Christian eyes,
completely out of bounds. This was especially so with regard to
the Mexicans, "a wretched people" but also one that had "abolished slavery" and did not "covet the lands of their neighbors."

Parker could never quite make up his mind how to situate
structural injustice within what certainly seemed, overall, a pro-
gressive-historical frame of American development. The spectacular literary example of Herman Melville comes to mind here as
well, a writer whose work revolved around this dilemma. Democracies, as O'Sullivan had succinctly emphasized, must "make their
conquests by moral agencies"; and thus, as we have seen, he recoded the Mexican events into a suitably moral narrative, while
others, such as the placid Emerson, merely resigned before the
inexorable workings of fate. The one injustice, however, that for
most of these intellectuals could never be transcended within the
frame was of course what they perceived to be the deeply un-
American institution of slavery. After the Compromise of 1850 and
the attendant Fugitive Slave Law, the eradication of slavery became a consuming interest for Parker and many others of the
New England intelligentsia. Yet, despite association with extreme

abolitionists, Parker conceived of racial difference in ways that were anything but egalitarian. Along with an extrordinarily broad spectrum of white opinion, North and South, he assumed blacks to be inherently inferior. Given Anglo-Saxon superiority, he also believed that, once emancipated, blacks would gradually fade away as a race.

In fact, by the 1840s virtually all destinarian thought entailed implicit or explicit references to "race." A proliferation of pseudoscientific theories of race in the Western world at the time generated, for obvious reasons, immense interest in the United States, thus adding fuel to the intensifying conflict over slavery and expansion. The new "science" featured such aspects as phrenological measurement of skulls and the conviction that blood determined race, making miscegenation and any mixing of white and black seem a deadly danger of contamination for the superior party. This discourse accomplished two things, in our context. First, it gave rise to a widening movement in the North not only to eliminate slavery but also to remove blacks from the republic of freedom through colonization schemes, curtailment of the rights of free blacks, or even the annexation of Texas as an aqueduct for "drainage" of blacks southward into the presumably more climatically suitable tropics. The Wilmot Proviso was only one expression of this vision. Second, it also produced an "internal" ranking of Caucasians to the effect that Anglo-Saxons were really the most advanced and vigorous within the white race as a whole. One popular way of putting this was through the old theme of "westward empire": the Aryan, Gothic peoples had been on the westward march for a good millennium and a half, and as any peek at the world map would indicate, the vanguard of that select series of tribes was the Anglo-Saxons. American westward domination, however, would differ from the British. For having recovered the original Anglo-Saxon liberties in their Revolution, the Americans were actually the more genuine article, untainted by the decadence of Norman aristocracy. The contrast was clear, therefore, between British colonial-aristocratic rule of Asia and the properly pure, American elimination of otherness in North America. The Anglo-Saxonism that had fascinated Jefferson experienced a revival in the mid-nineteenth century in more sinister guise. The meaning of "Anglo-Saxon" varied considerably, from the mythical pre-Norman purity to an identity of generic Americanized whiteness. In any case, "blots" and "mixture" would not be tolerated. Yet the census of 1850 showed some 3.6 million blacks, 3.2 million of whom were slaves. These Americans would not fade or go away. They have yet to fade or go away.

Let us now examine the conservative *American Whig Review*, whose changing response to expansionism is interesting because it foreshadows a new kind of thinking about destiny and empire, an empire of deterritorialized commerce. No particular line seems to have been set on expansionism at the outset, and the position taken in 1845 on California seemed oddly reminiscent of O'Sullivan's. There was even talk of "the manifest designs of Providence" and "the silent, resistless legislation of the Omnipotent Lawgiver" that "must, ere long, place California beneath other sovereignty." Asserting that Texas had been expropriated from the slothful Mexicans through "natural progress," the *American Whig Review* proposed the morally correct purchase of Alta California in the name of humanity. No "regeneration" of "this vast and magnificent region" was possible until the present people had been ousted.

The tone changed markedly when Daniel Dewey Barnard, former congressman from upstate New York, became chief editorialist in 1845. He was an orthodox, elitist Whig in favor of communitarian consolidation and opposed to territorial acquisitions, in which spirit he wrote hard-hitting critiques of Polk's war. To Barnard, it was an immoral aggression of the strong against the weak motivated by covetousness. For notions of manifest destiny he had nothing but contempt:

> They call it our "manifest destiny." We are not sure that this "manifest destiny" of our Republic stops short—in their imaginings—of absorbing the whole of North America. We are not sure that even South America is to escape. Their notion is that the Spanish race on this continent, and all others, must fade away before the face of the Anglo-Saxons, or rather of the Yankees, as the shadows fly before the coming light.

A real understanding of national purpose, on the contrary, had to be a product of moral continuity with the past. Otherwise the effect on the American nation would be truly dystopian:

> Contemplating this future, we behold all seas covered by our fleets; our garrisons hold the most important stations of commerce; an immense standing army maintains our possessions; our traders have become the richest, our demagogues the most powerful, and our people the most corrupt and flexible in the world.

This, today, seems a prediction of considerable historical insight. Meanwhile, however, the *Review* also published pieces with diametrically opposite implications. Thus, in March 1847, the Reverend H. W. Bellows held forth at some length on "The Destiny of the Country," what he took to be the "glorious plan" that Providence had in store for the new continent and the new race:

> It becomes a simple calculation, how soon, at this rate, we shall reach the Pacific ocean. And long before that time our cup must run over in the southern direction. That Mexico will ultimately fall a political prey, not to force, but to a superior population, insensibly oozing into her territories, changing her customs, and out-loving, out-trading, exterminating her weaker blood, we regard with as much certainty, as we do the final extinction of the Indian races, to which the mass of the Mexican population seem very little superior; and we have no reason to doubt that this country will not have doubled its three centuries of existence, before South America will speak the English tongue and submit to the civilization, laws and religion of the Anglo-Saxon race.

An unsigned piece two years later indicated a similarly "stupendous, startling future" under the auspices of the silent workings of the "Supreme Disposer," who wanted to create in North America "a scope for human energies of thought and will, such as has never yet been seen since the days before the flood," all of which would "draw the whole world around it and along with it in its

gigantic march." When this appeared in 1849, Europe was embroiled in a political crisis of the profoundest sort, so it was easy
perhaps to envision the American century a bit before its time.
It also appeared, of course, before the slavery issue took over the
political arena completely. Bellows originally emphasized in fact
that the bright prospects were predicated on first getting rid of
that huge blot, the institution of slavery. By 1849, too, Barnard
had left the *Review*; and as the article indicated, it took only a
moment after the end of the war for the *Review* to revert to older
views. Certainly, it was conceded, the war had been unjust; but
in the end the United States had paid decent money for the territories and the additions were "destined to make our country the
world's historical centre." Technological innovation would shrink
distances: "The barriers of time and space will be annihilated."
Marvelous commercial opportunities would open up:

> The trade of China and of a large portion of Asia must find
> its way across the western ocean to our Pacific shores, build-
> ing up great towns and cities there, and thence across to the
> Atlantic coast, there to meet the trade of Europe coming over
> the Atlantic on its western route.

Such dreams of the United States (or, more specifically, the Mississippi Valley) as the new gravitational center of trade and civilization had already appeared to Jefferson. It is worth noting, too,
that when Asa Whitney, originally a China merchant, initiated
the transcontinental railroad project in the early 1840s, he did so
with similar visions of a new age of commercial mediation between Europe and Asia, all for the ulterior purposes of Christian
civilization.

In the postwar odes is discernible a whole new theme in American nationalism, a quasi-imperial theme of speed, bustle, and
trade. Destiny would take a detour before this vision could come
into focus again, for slavery would not in fact disappear in the
facile manner that some of these Whig writers blithely took for
granted. The pioneering figure before the Civil War to recast territorial empire into a commercial, yet destinarian, register was William H. Seward. The Whig governor and subsequent senator from

New York became Lincoln's chief Republican rival in the 1850s and then his Secretary of State. But before pursuing the New Yorker, I want to say a word about his great model, John Quincy Adams, of whom indeed he wrote an early biography. Adams is a fascinating character here for several reasons. He played a larger role in the territorial gains than anyone except Jefferson and Polk; and he thought seriously about the process. Of deep continentalist persuasion, he was the principal author in 1823 of the Monroe Doctrine (wherein appeared a sentence with the two words "destiny" and "manifestation"). Yet U.S. expansionism took on a different aspect for him after—alone among ex-Presidents in American history—he was elected to Congress, where he became the most visible abolitionist in the country. Adams was one of the very few in 1846 to vote against appropriations for the Mexican War. His trajectory is illustrative.

Like his father, John Quincy Adams was a quintessential product of New England Puritanism, an archetype of selfless labor, discipline, devotion, internal repression. Born in the 1760s, he was the last politician for whom the Revolution was a living, existential fact. About the virtues and the righteousness of the original American project, he never harbored any doubts at all: "The whole continent of North America appears to be destined by Divine Providence to be peopled by one *nation*, speaking one language, professing one general system of religious and political principles, and accustomed to one general tenor of social usages and customs," he wrote to his father in 1811. Throughout his life, he held unswervingly to the conviction that American expansionism derived its legitimacy from the imperatives of the Old Testament. Nature, the providential configuration of space on earth, existed to be appropriated and improved upon for the glorification of God. Liberty in this regard was at once a power and a duty to labor for "ends of beneficence." Anything short of that was to break the promise and extinguish the legitimacy. Providence, then, had singled out the North American continent for the United States to realize its mission of improvement; this much was evident from a simple reading of the map, or "the finger of nature," as he paraphrased the Old Testament reference to the indicative "finger of God." Accordingly, Adams's roomy view in-

cluded at one point Cuba with its 600,000 slaves, bound by prox-
imity and political "gravitation," as he thought, to fall at some
stage into the bosom of the Union.

Subsequently, he had occasion in various contexts to follow
through on this geopolitical prophecy. Alone in Monroe's cabinet
he even went so far as to support Andrew Jackson's forays into
Florida against the Seminole Indians and the Spanish. Perhaps he
was blinded by the map, for he never saw any conflict here with
his absolute principles of Christian ethics and humanitarian notions of uplifting the world. Indeed, it took his miserable presidency in the mid-1820s and the subsequent deflation of domestic
improvement programs at the hands of that very same Jackson to
open his eyes (though he typically refused to recognize any
change in himself). By the 1830s, territorial gains were thus no
longer fulfillment of God's promise but chiefly an evil extension
of slavery, a disgraceful, tyrannical usurpation of the national purpose. This view earned him, not undeservedly, some southern
accusations of hypocrisy, for had he not in fact himself tried to
buy Texas even before Mexico had abolished slavery? Adams
could never satisfactorily respond. He could claim consistency in
the sense that his shift occurred only when he began to think of
the Union as qualitatively altered, as being well on the way to
becoming a slave power.

Debates on Texas annexation and the Mexican War offered
plenty of outlets for his savage sarcasm. On Oregon, however, his
stance recalled older views, never really relinquished. He had decided to push the "all of Oregon" line partly for tactical reasons,
since he was sure that Polk was using the northwestern claim to
muddy the waters around Texan slavery and so would back down
when push came to shove, as the President in fact also did. But
in principle, too, he thought Americans had a superior claim because they, far better than the British, would be able "to make
the wilderness blossom as the rose, to establish laws, to increase,
multiply, and subdue the earth, which we are commanded to do
by the first behest of God Almighty." However, Adams was willing
to compromise for the time being. Extension into Mexico, by contrast, was exportation of slavery into a free territory, thus historically retrograde and unnatural. Adams's understanding of history
was strictly teleological: deviations from the process of natural

unfolding were steps backward and therefore perverse. On these grounds, for example, he found reason to support the British in the Opium War against China, not because of the commodity in question but because, in wanting to keep opium out, the Chinese were refusing the Europeans equality of contract and exchange, thus assuming the feudal role of lord to the vassal—all of which would turn history back, something very unnatural indeed.

Adams's mixture of Christian and commercial ethics in a frame of progressive historical development exerted strong influence on Seward. But the latter was also a dialectical thinker of great sophistication and strategic insight in his own right. It has been his fate, however, to be remembered for his famous "folly," the secret purchase of Alaska in 1867 for the outrageous price of $7 million. Not even President Andrew Johnson had been informed. Seward's vision of a flexible commercial empire, at any rate, was as stringently liberal as could be found at the time.

"The nation," he instructed the Senate in 1853, "that draws the most materials and provisions from the earth, fabricates the most, and sells the most of productions and fabrics to foreign nations, must be, and will be, the great power of the earth." This was his basic geo-economic premise. Command over "the ultimate empire of the ocean," the only "real empire," was therefore what mattered. Britain offered a glaringly obvious lesson to this effect. Laggard by comparison, the United States nevertheless had enormous potential for emulation. Here Seward was far less impressed by expanding imperial borders than, figuratively speaking, the development of steam power. Though doubtless Christian traders and civilizers, the British had become locked into the old pattern of European colonialism, subjugators forced, as it were, to rely on force. By contrast, freedom of economic activity and protection of natural rights within a constitutional system, the two ideal and ideological features of American life, put the United States in an excellent position to compete for the empire of the future. Unrestrained by old irrationalities, the nation would *attract* instead of subjugate: open borders and increasing commerce coupled with respect for local autonomy would draw the foreign inescapably into the most advanced form of Western civilization and hence also serve to elevate.

Seward, along with so many other nineteenth-century liberals,

believed that "commerce has largely taken the place of war," that
commerce would produce "influence" as well as an exchange of
commodities, all for the immediate benefit of the advanced and
the long-term benefit of the retrograde. This may seem a rosy
vision (though popular again today) but Seward was anything but
complacent about the strategic imperatives of his new geo-
economic system. The United States needed massive development of its infrastructure, better internal social cohesion (hence
the need to abolish immoral and divisive slavery), vigorous moves
to secure worldwide shipping stations and open corridors of trade.
New York he envisaged as the supreme financial center of a global
trading system, the core currency of which would of course be
the dollar. Since he was convinced that the decisive area of future
commercial competition lay in Asia, the acquisition of Hawaii
made sense, as did the projection of an isthmian canal and, less
obviously, the purchase of Alaska.

In his more rhetorical moments, Seward sometimes conjured
up images of aggressive continental expansion, but generally he
took a dim view of the "growing passion for territorial aggrandizement." It tended to generate "gross disregard for justice and
humanity." Rewriting history for tactical purposes, however, he
presented this "passion" as incidental, as a minor key, in a national development otherwise marked by peace and order, reform
and cultivation. This was a necessary act of rewriting, for his geo-
economic design had to fit into a universal view of Christianity
and progress in world history. The aspiration, then, was more than
a vulgar empire of commerce: his plan was an attempt to follow
His plan, and neither was that simple. Ideology and culture
("moral forces" in Seward's terminology) did not advance in a
straight line; nor indeed did material power. They only moved
forward "subject to conflict and reaction." Moral and civic criteria
determined whether this would be an upward spiral: "A nation
deficient in intelligence and virtue is an ignoble one, and no ignoble race can enlarge or even retain empire." Though slavery
amounted to a sizable deficiency, the United States still demonstrated such virtue and potential for "advancing the welfare of
mankind." The absolute standard, however, was the degree to
which agents served the providential design. For history in the

end was nothing but the divine principle unfolding in the here and now according to the "supreme law" of the "equality of nations, of races, and of men." The United States, then, "would disclose the secret of the ultimate regeneration and reunion of human society throughout the world." In other words, it was the manifest end of history.

Alas, Seward's imaginative design came to naught because of the Civil War, which forced him as Secretary of State to deal with wholly different matters. Afterward he failed to acquire Hawaii, but through the Burlingame Treaty of 1868 he secured the importation of Chinese labor to build the transcontinental railroads. When he died in 1872, it was domestic development and colonization that dominated politics, leaving schemes of American destiny in the world to the marginal few. Toward the end of the century, when Seward's themes were revived, it was ironically often in a *militarized and territorialized form* that he, along with Adams, would have found historically retrograde.

(5)

If Seward's Christian-commercial vision was one possible mutation of manifest destiny in the 1850s, the nationalist movement of Young America and the many military expeditions of the filibusters represented two other possibilities. At the ideological level, both were related to the deepening crisis over slavery and thus in a way they were symbolic resolutions of something that could not be resolved.

The brief ascendancy of Young America was immediately linked to the political upheavals of 1848 in Europe as well as to the role members of the group came to play in the internal struggles of the Democratic Party over issues and patronage. Nationality and democracy had figured centrally in these European revolutions, causing reverberations of sympathy in the United States. Beyond sympathy, however, few were prepared to go. Loud demands for more active solidarity and intervention emanated chiefly from a circle of Democrats known then as "Young Americans," young because their targets included "old fogies" within their own party. Stephen Douglas of Illinois became their

national figure, and support stemmed generally from the same
areas of ardent expansionism as in the 1840s; that is, northern
midwestern states and New York. Nothing much came of the
enterprise, which was long on bombast and short on specifics.
The Democratic administrations of Pierce and Buchanan were
strongly expansionist themselves, by inclination and also as a response to the domestic crisis; but their posture was restricted to
the old method of annexation in proximate areas.

Members of the New York group, notably O'Sullivan, were engaged in various filibustering operations as well. The term comes
from Dutch and Spanish terms for "free booty" and indicated
swashbuckling attempts on the part of Americans, sometimes together with indigenous exiles, to take over areas or whole regimes
in the Caribbean basin and Mexico. A missionary belief in the
blessings of American democracy was combined here, not necessarily cynically, with various schemes and intrigues for personal
enrichment. Filibustering continued, sometimes with tacit Administration support, from the late 1840s to the Civil War. Thus
William Walker, the most notorious and certainly most indefati-
gable filibuster, managed to take over Nicaragua for a while. Still,
not a single stable result was achieved by these piratical spirits.

Most of them were southerners. For the first time, expansionism flavored by the language of manifest destiny became popular
in the South, indicative of the sharpening sectionalism of the
1850s. Disagreement over the spoils of the Mexican War exacerbated this process immeasurably. While Calhoun and many southern Whigs had opposed simple destinarian aggrandizement, the
extension of slavery and Americanism (of the southern sort) into
tropical regions, regions now reclassified as paradisical, began to
seem attractive to the cramped southern perception. So it did to
the crisis-ridden Democratic Party. Cuba particularly became an
object of desire, and both Pierce and Buchanan tried hard to pro-
cure it. All sorts of reasons for its annexation could be adduced
but perhaps the basic one was the fear that Spain would eman-
cipate the slaves and hence cause the emergence of yet another
black republic in addition to Santo Domingo (Haiti). Since it became popular to think that democracy, inherently active and
restless, was "naturally" expansive and needed to grow to stay

healthy, one could argue that the only viable route lay to the south. Phantasmagorical visions of easy annexation proliferated. The tropical republics were ripe and ready, said one southern congressman. He had learned nothing from the Mexican War: "With swelling hearts and suppressed impatience they await our coming, and with joyous shouts of 'Welcome! welcome!' will they receive us."

That pronouncement was made on the eve of the Civil War, the greatest single conflagration in the century between the Napoleonic Wars and the First World War. It was the collapse, it may have seemed, of any single-minded ideas of American destiny. Traditional themes of the right to rebellion, independence, and liberty were redeployed in the service of the Confederate cause and every aspect of American ideology was put into contestation. But the course of the war soon allowed the victorious North to regain its destinarian footing. There was a great deal of apocalyptic talk about Armageddon, about the eradication of sinful slavery as the final battle. The United States would be born again, "a mountain of holiness for the dissemination of light and purity to all nations," as one Reverend in Philadelphia decreed. With the end in sight, the Unionist cause could be interpreted as divine vindication. Thus the Civil War revitalized confidence in the American mission, now properly national and northern.

III

BLESSINGS OF CIVILIZATION
1865–1914

One of the most common images after the Civil War was originally an advertisement. Painted in naive style by John Gast
and entitled "American Progress, or Manifest Destiny," it was first
used in 1872 to promote a book called *New Overland Tourist and
Pacific Coast Guide*. At center stage appears a bright, angelic
woman allegorically named "Star of Empire." She holds an educational book in one hand and a telegraph wire in the other. Facing west, the ethereal figure floats toward the Rocky Mountains.
Behind her, at the far right, is the Brooklyn Bridge (at that time
under construction). The east is light, enlightened, and civilized;
the west is dark, awaiting the illumination brought by Star of
Empire and her surrounding cast of settlers, stagecoaches, and
railroads. In the murky west, giving way to the inevitable movement of the forces of light, are a sorry-looking group of Indians
and wild beasts.

Bishop Berkeley's poetic stanza as modified by John Quincy
Adams had thus achieved a fitting apotheosis in the new postbellum world of advertising. But the motif also indicated the
actual course of expansionary efforts in the twenty-five years following Seward's Alaskan "folly." For this would be a period when
expansion remained largely within, a movement into the acquired
areas of the continent coupled with rapid industrialization in the
older, already settled parts. Territorial acquisitions of note would

have to await the late 1890s when another war, the Spanish-American War of 1898, as in the 1840s a fairly painless one for the United States, landed the nation with colonies and protectorates outside the continent proper.

This imperial departure was controversial. Critical voices wondered pointedly how it could be squared with American traditions, how a postcolonial nation could accept the role of colonizer. In the ensuing debate about national purpose, talk of manifest destiny reappeared in full force, as did some of the arguments of the 1840s. But conceptions of self could no longer be forged with the same ease as half a century earlier, when there was still the luxury of simply imagining the future as homogeneous and removed: more of the same territory, more of the same people, at a safe distance from old and dastardly Europe. The outside world of the 1890s was far closer both in time and space, appeared in fact ominously crowded and competitive. The setting was now different and so, ultimately, was the framing of destiny.

Four interrelated shifts stand out here: (1) the other Western powers were frenetically gobbling up territory in Africa and Asia and legitimating their activity in terms of empire and advancing civilization, hence forcing Americans to relate their own enterprise directly to Old World models; (2) as geographical destiny ceased to be continental and "American," its spatial character became unclear, less manifest; (3) extracontinental expansion also put into question, at least momentarily, the ideal of unblemished U.S. homogeneity; (4) Christianity lost *explanatory* ground to various modernizing, scientific, and pseudoscientific discourses, though it remained the reigning ideology of cohesion. These four developments attenuated received ideas of identity and destiny. Where and under what circumstances would "the United States" end? What in fact was it? And how might the exceptional United States be distinguished from Europe, now that one was embarking on what seemed a career in colonialism? It was in response to such queries that the American mission was reconceived as a kind of civilizational imperialism under Anglo-Saxon impress.

Before we proceed to that, however, we must have a better account of the American state and how it related to the rapidly changing geopolitical environment of the late nineteenth century.

(2)

The American state had always been weak. To some notable European observers, it seemed not even to exist. Exist it most certainly did, as we have seen, but with very little domestic agency and autonomy, which was why it proved incapable of resolving the slavery issue. Federalism itself, in fact, had made secession fairly easy to envision. After all, these were already "states," juridically separate entities in which the federal government had only a marginal presence anyway. The resultant Civil War had devastated the South and temporarily strengthened the federal state because of the mobilization, the vast expropriation of southern property, and the ensuing occupation. When the war ended in 1865, the North had a million men under arms; and important sections of the ruling Republican Party were intending to wipe out southern separatism forever by means of radical social surgery. By the mid-1870s, however, the army had dwindled to fewer than thirty thousand men, its central operation once again reduced to securing the western frontier for settlement. The effort to remake the South had fizzled out.

The northern victory did eradicate once and for all the notion of double sovereignty and made the Union indisputably a union —the United States ceased to be plural and became an "it." The federal government now also fulfilled a new and important redistributive function through the sizable apparatus of veteran pensions. Thus there could be no return to antebellum conditions. Yet the state retreated as an institution and the dominant forces in North and South alike supported this well into the 1890s. Economically exploited and stagnant, the South began after Reconstruction to develop an apartheid regime, disenfranchising in the process not only the newly emancipated blacks but also many poor whites. In such circumstances, invigoration of federal authority entailed no virtues; it created visions of the hated Yankee occupation that had finally ended in 1877. Northern capital, on the other hand, had achieved its basic aims: the opening up of national markets, a protectionist tariff system, massive subsidies in the form of land grants to railroads, the creation of a resourceful indigenous system of finance tied to, yet also independent from, the federal government. Henceforth its interest lay in blocking any political attempts to circumscribe the capitalist liberty to expand and make profits. Nothing illustrates the direction of events better than the strange career of the Fourteenth Amendment: intended to endow former slaves with citizenship, by the 1890s it had been converted into a legal weapon for big corporations to combat emerging unions, the existence of which was ruled to violate the civil rights of said corporations, which had been defined by obliging courts as "persons."

Exercising the right to free enterprise generated clashes with labor remarkable for their frequency and violence. It is instructive here to note that the Pinkerton Detective Agency in the 1890s was larger than the U.S. Army. The Pinkertons were chiefly engaged in labor repression in the form of intelligence gathering and physical intimidation. Corporations, in some cases, also had private armies. When, in open confrontation, these proved insufficient, industrialists could call upon various state militias and sometimes even federal troops. In such a congenial situation there was little interest on the part of employers in negotiation and compromise. My point is twofold: the repressive apparatuses of the state were small but adequate to the task at hand, and that task was internal "order," not geopolitical confrontation.

In the political sphere, the closely balanced Republicans and Democrats fought hotly contested elections utterly devoid of fundamental issues. Disenfranchisement gradually undermined the Republican position in the South, turning the region into a one-party system. Add clientism and boss-dominated machines in the urban North and it stands to reason that any kind of reform, at least at the federal level, was an uphill battle. This, at any rate, was the bitter lesson for the genteel, bourgeois reformers of the Northeast who were so scandalized by corruption and crass materialism, so incensed by the glaring decline of standards in the public sector. It was from the ranks of these "mugwump" reformers that many of the anti-imperialist leaders of the 1890s would emerge.

Overshadowing all this and severely limiting any widespread mobilization for reform was the anarchic and staggering economic growth in virtually every domain. Infusion of cheap labor through mass immigration, technological innovation, abundance of land and resources, ample availability of capital, markets at home and abroad, and few domestic boundaries or political controls to consider: these factors propelled the United States by the 1890s to the leading position in the world in both manufacturing and agriculture. American competition was by then serious enough to make European observers deeply worried. Yet foreign trade was overall far less important to the U.S. economy than to the competitors. The engine of growth was domestic.

With no external threats and possessing vast internal territory to be exploited, the ruling classes had no reason to be eager about colonies and geopolitics. There was little competence in international power politics and not much need for it. Foreign relations in the postbellum period thus lapsed into comparative obscurity. Territorial expansionism, at least southward, was still tainted by previous ties, real and imagined, to "slave power." There was, to be sure, a good deal of economic interest and penetration in the Caribbean. But when civil war broke out in Cuba in 1868, a conflict that would last a decade, there was no serious attempt to get involved. And though the Dominican Republic seemed available for annexation in the 1870s, President Grant could not mobilize enough support for it. The perennial project of an isthmian canal, meanwhile, was discussed with renewed urgency in light of the success of the Suez Canal; but nothing materialized. Minor proddings northward to make the Canadians join the Union petered out. By the early 1890s reputable opinion-makers could propose, half seriously, the abolition of the State Department on the grounds that it was an extravagant joke.

Only one development broke the pattern, a sizable naval armament program that was begun in the 1880s. Its origins, however, were again largely domestic. For the federal government was running a surplus, and navies could be justified in terms of steel purchases, protection of shipping, and general defense in a shrinking world. Naming battleships after such unlikely states as Iowa and Indiana ensured political support. The program would later get a tremendous boost from successes in the Spanish-American War, and naval expansion was to be sustained until the end of Theodore Roosevelt's presidency. Indeed, when he sent the Great

White Fleet around the world in 1908, it represented a navy second only to Britain's. Yet, as mentioned, the early impetus had come from within, not from any immediate geopolitical concerns.

The period after 1870 was thus one of internal colonization and development under the aegis of northern capital, sanctioned by a thoroughly compliant court system and underpinned by a state providing repression and corrupt party machines with sustaining patronage. The American state (or states, rather, since it was a disarticulated series of levels and institutions) evinced in this regard three "discrepancies" compared to its European counterparts: (1) its infrastructural power was much more limited; (2) while European powers were taking the first steps toward an interventionist, "social" state, the United States retained a thoroughly entrenched laissez-faire system, heavily weighted in favor of big capital; and (3) its external posture showed, until the 1890s, none of the geopolitical capabilities that so obsessed its European peers. To put it a bit vulgarly, while others were busy constructing alliances and empires all over the globe and buying off the domestic opposition, the United States was busy constructing the most efficient economic juggernaut in the world, but one notably turned mostly inward.

What is more, these discrepancies were widening, and some influential Americans had begun to worry about it, especially the geopolitical aspect. Traditional "isolationism" was for them nothing praiseworthy; it was a liability, a *gap*. The prescription then was to narrow the gap by becoming more "European." Others, however, had a completely different reaction. For those unsettled by the deep domestic changes there was a growing suspicion that "America" was about to fall into the world and become one of the multitude, beset with the social problems and class conflicts associated with the Old World. The United States seemed in danger of losing its blessed exemption from history, its exceptionalism. Overseas empire could only mean a huge step toward the abyss. Because of our central concern with territorial expansionism, this imperial and geopolitical dimension deserves a further comment.

Many nineteenth-century liberals in the Anglophone world liked to think that economic "globalization" equaled interdependence, which in turn would equal increasing civilization and peace. In fact, however, industrialization accelerated within a framework of increasing protectionism and hardening nation-state boundaries. Thus it became inextricably tied to militarization and an intensifying arms race, especially in the naval sector. Industrial technology increased vastly the potential lethality of warfare, while expanded standing armies underscored the pronounced *nationalist* implications of this new situation. The late nineteenth century brought about a crescendo in the invention of ancient national traditions. Thus the nation-state, historically a contingent form of capitalism and a relatively recent one at that, assumed the guise of a natural end of development, the last stage of civilization.

Antagonism within this essentially European order (Japan entering in the 1890s) came to the fore in intermittent diplomatic crises and the building of alliances; but the more salient experience, at least to contemporaries, was the explosive imperial expansion. Between 1875 and 1914, one quarter of the world was claimed as colonies. Britain alone added 4 million square miles. European empires had of course existed for a long time, but only after 1870 was there a sustained attempt to turn the rapidly accumulating colonial possessions into a formal system. It was then, for example, that Queen Victoria officially added the title of Empress. In the imperialist "scramble for Africa," as the expression went, and in similar rivalries elsewhere, expectations of economic advantage played a significant role. Much less by way of profitable commerce and extraction of raw materials actually issued in the real world than expected; but once the race for territory had begun it took on strategic considerations. It became part of a globalized game among Great Powers. The United States, though an economic powerhouse, was in this respect still outside the range of serious players. The "civilized world," in sum, was developing into a configuration of national and potentially nationalist entities with colonial appendages and protectionist economies. Unlike, for example, the transnational aristocracy of earlier Europe, classes thus became increasingly rooted in the purely domestic sphere and its colonial extension. They confronted each other as nation-state against nation-state, empire against empire, alliance against alliance.

The effects were several. *Ideologically*, two convictions followed. First and most generally, "the West" was seen as obviously superior in every way because, equally obviously, it ruled the world; and it was justified in ruling the world because it was superior. New theories of evolution and race offered scientific confirmation of this circular idea. Second, war was understood by dominant circles to be rational policy. For war would either be short and decisive (witness Bismarck's successes in the 1860s and '70s); or, because massive armaments and civilized solidarity within the West made hostilities unthinkable there, it would be used *only against the barbaric outside*, by definition a zone of anarchy legitimately subject to forceful imposition of rational order as a step toward civilization. *Politically*, the uneven, gradual inclusion of wider segments of the populations into the established order reinforced the old privacy and secrecy that had always typified geopolitics in the European state system. This seems odd at first, but the domestic nature of the popularization process actually served to keep foreign policy from public view, except in moments of crisis. Jingoism and superficial engagement, predicated on the advent of mass literacy and mass newspapers, could then easily be whipped up, to the point of overtaking events. War in the popular mind became what William James derogatorily but rightly called an "exciting kind of *sport*."

Mass participation in politics had occurred in the United States long before this period; and, as noted, there was nothing much in postbellum times to keep from view in the first place. But James Polk and the Mexican War had shown how the Executive might use the conduct of foreign relations for its own purposes when the circumstances were right. The effects could be absurd. In 1889, for example, the United States almost ended up in war with Germany because of a conflict over tiny Samoa in the Pacific, a conflict that Secretary of State James Blaine was able to carry on largely at his leisure. In 1895, Grover Cleveland and his Secretary of State, Richard Olney, provided further evidence of manipulative power when they picked a quarrel with Great Britain over an essentially trivial question regarding the boundary between Venezuela and British Guiana. They informed London, much to popular acclaim, that the United States had the right to decide the issue because it was, to use Olney's formulation, "prac-

tically sovereign on this continent." That indelicate and erroneous formulation, a loose interpretation of the Monroe Doctrine,
rubbed the British very much the wrong way. Cleveland and Olney themselves, meanwhile, were thoroughly unsettled by the instant success of their public excursion into power politics. A
compromise saving face all around was worked out, ultimately
possible because of the quiet but long-standing British policy of
appeasement toward the United States: more important things
were at stake outside the Americas. Three years later, indeed, the
popular spirit was suddenly vociferously pro-British, as London
had made a considerable effort of support during the Spanish-
American War. To that crucial moment of expansionism we may
now turn.

(3)

In 1893, the United States had been hit by the most severe economic depression it had ever experienced. Because of underlying
deflationary tendencies going back to the 1870s, the widespread
political discontent arising from the crisis came to center inordi-
nately on currency questions, particularly on the monetarization
of silver. Forces led by William Jennings Bryan committed the
Democratic Party to this position, but in 1896, in the first crucial
election since 1860, he lost to William McKinley, a less-than-
spectacular machine politician from Ohio, or so it seemed. The
election initiated a period of Republican hegemony in national
politics that would last till the election of Franklin D. Roosevelt
in 1932, the Wilsonian interlude having been made possible only
through the Republican split in 1912.

Throughout but also beyond the depression, worries that the
system would not be able to cope spread beyond the mugwumps
into the mainstream. The dislocations were indeed massive: pres-
sures of urbanization, immigration from new and unrecognizable
places in southeastern Europe (20 million immigrants arrived between 1870 and 1910), labor and farmer unrest, populist and socialist agitation, giant corporations and trusts, and other swiftly
emerging, unfamiliar phenomena. The cherished frontier had already been consigned to the past by the census of 1890. What

remained, and powerfully so, was Frederick Jackson Turner's famous thesis, articulated in 1893, that the frontier had shaped the very essence of the (inheritable) American character. But Turner's argument merely underlined in the popular mind that the United States was no longer a society of sturdy pioneers. If American identity was indeed the process of pioneering the frontier and the latter had ceased to exist, what sort of new form might that identity then assume? Small wonder that the preeminent literary genre from the late 1880s to the turn of the century was utopian fiction, featuring a paradoxical desire to change the American present fundamentally in order to make it into something once again stable and unchanging, or at any rate into what was believed to have been something stable and unchanging.

In this general climate, expansionism returned to the political agenda, with a vengeance. It had made an early, pre-depression appearance in 1892–93 when American sugar interests in Hawaii had engineered independence, followed in time-honored fashion by calls for American annexation. But Grover Cleveland, the incoming Democratic President, had blocked it. In 1898, by contrast, the annexation of Hawaii sailed through Congress easily because of the war with Spain. It was through that war, then, that elements of similarity with the Western "model" came strongly to the fore: executive secrecy and manipulation against a backdrop of intense but momentary interest among a largely uninformed public; an imperial move to colonize overseas territories; a splashing entry, apparently, into the world of Great Powers. Thus, in 1898, the United States seized Cuba, Puerto Rico, Guam, Wake Island, and Manila in the Philippines; the following year, a bloody colonial war of subjugation began in the Philippines that would last until 1902. Washington also declared the "Open Door" policy with regard to China and followed it up by sending marines to Beijing to quell the so-called Boxer Rebellion. The coda of this extraordinary reorientation occurred in 1903 when Theodore Roosevelt assisted Panamian separatists to break away from Colombia in exchange for American rights to extraterritoriality. The isthmian canal could finally be built.

The complexities of these events are beyond my scope; but an account of the Spanish-American War and its immediate aftermath is useful. The origins of this war lay in the revival in 1895 of the Cuban rebellion against the oppressive Spanish colonial authority. A coalition for national liberation, spanning the whole range of indigenous classes, was formed. The Spanish regime, on its part, decided to launch a last, all-out effort to preserve its rule over this remaining, profitable colony. The brutalities of the ferocious conflict turned it into an American issue in the highly charged political climate of that moment. Press lords William Randolph Hearst and Joseph Pulitzer, locked in a circulation war, made Cuba a feature story through continuous, graphic accounts of Spanish cruelty. Expressions of solidarity, moreover, from the oppositional silver forces resulted in demands for, at minimum, American recognition of rebel belligerency. Cleveland, a conservative gold Democrat, had no interest in pursuing the issue, maintaining instead a policy of neutrality that served in fact to support the Spanish. Business interests in general also opposed any potentially disturbing action.

Nothing was known about McKinley's views on the matter when he came into the White House. Insofar as he had any, he refused to divulge them. Unlike Cleveland, he proved selectively favorable to annexationism. Surprisingly little has been learned about his thinking since. He left few documentary traces and stuck to his own counsels. He was known (wrongly) by his opponents as a mere tool of Republican boss rule and (rightly) for his quasi-religious attachment to protectionism. Outwardly he continued Cleveland's line, but privately, during the summer of 1897, he peremptorily informed the Spanish government that the imbroglio was having a detrimental effect on the American recovery. In fact, he was open to purchasing or annexing the island. Spain, under a new, more liberal regime in the fall, responded to the crisis with various autonomy solutions. These met with no success. In early 1898, McKinley sent the battleship *Maine* to Havana to protect American interests, a mostly symbolic move that ended in the notorious, fatal explosion (most likely an accident). War eventually ensued after the President, cautious as always, had procrastinated and left it up to Congress to make the final decision. Conservative opinion on the eastern seaboard, accused of crass and heartless materialism, finally swung around to supporting war.

War, in fact, was probably unnecessary since the Spanish government had informed McKinley of its desire to settle preponderantly on his terms; but this he kept largely to himself. It was, in any case, an immensely popular war because it was experienced as a humanitarian effort, and it turned out to be short. Splendid it was not, on the other hand, at least not for the amateurish army, most of which never made it out of the country. Among those left behind were William Jennings Bryan and his Nebraska Guard. The excitable Teddy Roosevelt, however, was able to bully his way onto a ship with his Rough Riders. The navy did well. In accordance with existing contingency plans but to the great surprise of the public, the Pacific Squadron made the initial, decisive attack on the Spanish fleet in the Philippines.

When Spain capitulated in July 1898, however, the United States was physically in control only of the southeastern section of Cuba, a beachhead in Puerto Rico, and the environs of Manila. This crucial fact was ignored in the peace negotiations with Spain later in the fall. McKinley, having tested the waters thoroughly, had decided by then to opt for annexation. Hawaii had already been accepted as a territory of the Union during the summer. In the case of Cuba, McKinley's hands were tied by the Teller Amendment, attached by Congress to the war authorization in order to make clear that there was no "intention to exercise sovereignty, jurisdiction, or control, except for the pacification" of the island. Since then, it had been discovered that the Cuban rebels were a lot blacker (meaning less "civilized") than anticipated and thus in need of extensive tutelage. "Pacification" nevertheless went relatively smoothly because, with Spain out of the way, the internal contradictions of the Cuban anticolonials could be exploited. Thus, in 1901, the island became nominally independent under U.S. protection, conceding a naval base (Guantanamo) in perpetuity and American rights to intervene whenever order was deemed under threat. Five years later the marines were indeed back; and Cuba was well on its way to becoming an American sugar plantation. As for Puerto Rico, there was no Teller Amendment and no one made much noise when it was appropriated. Its population, generally pro-Spanish, had no means of resisting. It was transformed into a protectorate, legally modeled after the British crown colony of Hong Kong. A century later, a protectorate it largely remains.

Annexing and pacifying the Philippines was an altogether different kettle of fish: seven thousand miles away, a myriad of islands, peoples, and languages, and, most dauntingly, an indigenous nationalist movement under arms with no intention of letting the United States assume a sovereignty it did not physically possess. Domestic opposition in the United States, not surprisingly, was also at its strongest against imperial rule here. The peace treaty was ratified by the Senate in February 1899 with a margin of one vote. At the same time, there began a war of subjugation that would, directly or indirectly, cause the death of some 200,000 Filipinos and involve, throughout the three years it lasted, no less than 127,000 U.S. soldiers, led by officers with suitable experience of Indian warfare at home. The final, victorious campaign against the nationalists was headed by General Arthur MacArthur, who thus initiated what would be a long family presence in the islands. Lacking any class of colonial administrators, however, the United States had to rely on indigenous forces to run the place, thus creating not only a "nationalized" client class but also, ironically, the basis for the future Philippine nation as such. In the 1930s Congress decided that the islands would become independent fifteen years thereafter, chiefly because domestic economic interests were clamoring for protection against Philippine imports.

After this sketch of elementary events, we are in a position to follow the manner in which they were understood and debated, spatially and temporally, in the context of destinarian thinking. I shall begin with an account of four major figures of intellectual and political influence who appeared in the period before the Spanish-American War. All of them were later to express some doubts about the wisdom of the war, or about the specific territorial extension that followed; but they offer a good view of the late-nineteenth-century discourses that sustained prevailing ideologies of expansionism in the name of destiny and civilizational imperialism.

(4)

An enormously popular work of nonfiction toward the end of the
century was a curious tract by the Reverend Josiah Strong, *Our
Country*. It appeared in 1885 and through numerous editions went
on to sell some 175,000 copies, an astonishing figure for what was
actually a fund-raiser for the Christian Home Missions. Strong
introduced a religious version of manifest destiny that was also
imperialist at a moment when the old continentalist imagination
was beginning to dry up. Outside the church, similar projections
were put forth along more scholarly lines by such intellectuals as
John Fiske and John Burgess. Meanwhile, in a different but related register, Captain Alfred Mahan provided the emergent navalism with an ideological foundation, a destinarian vision of
American geopolitics of the seas. This quartet, then, will set a
certain discursive range for the following debate.

Strong was central in the new interdenominational movement
devoted to conquering (a term then much in vogue) glaring social
ills. Thus he embodied three important strands of late-nineteenth-
century U.S. Protestantism: "liberal" theology; mission at home
and abroad; and the social gospel. The first was essentially a rein-
vention of natural theology for the purpose of responding to advances in natural science and history: God and history were thus
fused into a design of progressive, linear evolution of the fittest
(more about which below). Missionary activity, a defining trait of
American church life, reached an organizational peak toward the
end of the century: at home because of the need to maintain
one's position amid the new urban realities of aliens, Romanism,
corruption, and filth; abroad because of the urgent desire to
spread the blessings of the Word to non-Christian, uncivilized areas. Indeed, Christian missionaries were the one consistently "expansionist" feature of American foreign relations after the Civil
War: there were boundaries to be crossed and spaces to be
conquered. The social gospel, finally, was the reformist element
in this system: things needed to be remedied, redeemed, regenerated. Seen from that angle, Strong was a direct precursor of the
wider reformism of the "Progressive Era" after the turn of the
century.

Our Country took the form of an updated jeremiad and apocalyptic scenario. Time, argued Strong, was accelerating (as evidenced by improved transportation and global commerce) toward what seemed the final moment, "the final competition of the races." God had given Anglo-Saxon civilization in general and the United States in particular a command: Christianize and civilize the world or face divine retribution. Providentially blessed with resources and a vigorous population, the United States now showed ominous signs of degeneracy. American civilization, that is, the Anglo-Saxon sense of liberty and the "pure" form of Christianity, was imperiled. Yet Strong took comfort in the fact that the "mighty Anglo-Saxon race" was on the march, ruling "more than one-third of the earth's surface, and more than one-fourth of its people." Stupendous growth at home, meanwhile, indicated that Anglo-Saxons eventually would outnumber all other civilized peoples.

Within Anglophone civilization, it was clear too that God had commissioned the United States, the westward empire, as the future leader. It had already achieved the lead in material wealth and population, as well as the highest degree of Anglo-Saxonism and true Christianity. Since there were no more Western continents remaining, it seemed that God had been "training the Anglo-Saxon race" for the historical climax. The "powerful race" would "move down upon Mexico, down upon Central and South America, out upon the islands of the sea, over upon Africa and beyond." The result, inevitably, would be "extinction for the inferior races," chiefly through the sheer overwhelming force of "vitality and civilization" rather than physical extermination. "God's final and complete solution of the dark problem of heathenism among many inferior peoples" was thus "to dispossess the many weaker races, assimilate others, and mold the remainder." Nothing less then the destiny of the world being at stake, it was imperative for American Christians to choose righteousness and not pervert one's given purpose by falling into materialistic atheism and other temptations. So America would realize its anointed purpose as "God's right arm in his battle with the world's ignorance and oppression and sin."

Roughly contemporaneously with Strong, John Fiske and John Burgess introduced a similar theme of civilizational imperialism

—though the word "imperialism" was often shunned. Their vocabularly was less apocalyptic and more historical, though the plot remained Christian. Fiske, historian and also one of the earliest evolutionists in the United States, chose "manifest destiny" as one of three central themes when he was to introduce American political ideas to the English in 1880. History was for him, as for so many others in this epoch, a dualistic struggle between conquering civilization and retreating barbarism, an unfolding zerosum game bound to end, as he said, in "a sabbath of perpetual peace." What had originally been a tiny, bright spot of civilization had thus expanded, necessarily by violent means, against the barbaric societies, till now, happily, the battle was practically over. The advent of Anglo-dominated America had actually been the decisive moment here, eliminating serious geopolitical enemies on the continent (the Catholic French) and henceforth offering the world a unique laboratory for the development of the most advanced English ideas. It was Fiske's "moderate" estimate that Anglo-America, by the year 2000, would "number at least six or seven hundred millions." By then Africa would have followed suit, turning into "a mighty nation of English descent, and covered with populous cities and flourishing farms, with railroads and telegraphs and other devices of civilization as yet undreamed of." When the undeveloped world was finally "English in its language, in its political habits and traditions, and to a predominant extent in the blood of its people," the end would have been reached and the perpetual sabbath of civilized peace begun. (Substitute "capitalism" for "civilization" here and the story is identical to present-day stories about the rise and final victory of "free enterprise.") At that stage, too, the older, non-English civilizations would have had to relinquish their militarism in competition with industrially superior Anglo states. Consequently, the conditions for a global, federated version of United States would be at hand.

The structure of Fiske's narrative was directly taken from his English friend Herbert Spencer. This erstwhile railway engineer is now not readily remembered, but he was the single most influential Anglophone thinker of the latter part of the nineteenth century. A proponent of all-embracing theory of the grandest sort, Spencer thought all societies necessarily evolved from barbarism to civilization through three distinct stages: the first, anarchic savagery, evolved into despotic militarism, which in turn became industrial capitalism. All three stages, however, also existed simultaneously, since different parts of the world had advanced more than others. Peace would reign once the final stage had been generalized, because the state would largely have withered away under the efficient policy of laissez-faire. Militarism, then, was historically regressive. Spencer, therefore, came to oppose the British Boer War, just as some of his American counterparts came to oppose the Spanish-American War. At the same time, he believed strongly in the virtue of struggle and "the survival of the fittest," the evocative phrase he invented in response to Darwin. Struggle, for Spencer, was the very essence of progressive evolution, biological and historical. Any state intervention, especially welfare reform, in the advanced stage was hopelessly self-defeating as it made the lower classes lazier and prevented the invigoration of desire and enterprise overall. Society and people alike needed to exercise to be fit, to use their capabilities to the full; otherwise productive organs (as opposed to the state) would literally wither away. When laissez-faire capitalism had become universal, struggle would consist in peaceful competition. Life at the end of history would express the rationality of capitalism itself.

As evolutionism, this position must be distinguished from Darwin's, since late-nineteenth-century thought is often characterized as "Social Darwinist" when, if anything, it was actually Spencerian with a touch of vulgarized Darwin: advocacy, on the basis of biological models, of laissez-faire and "the survival of the fittest." Darwin's real originality, however, lay not in the notion of evolution—scarcely a new idea—but in the theory of natural selection. This theory claims that individual members of a species adapt to changing environments with varying success depending on how well they fit these circumstances. "Fitness," therefore, has nothing inherently to do with bigness or strength or any preexisting value of "good." Darwin's theory is neither teleological, nor linear, nor hierarchical. Indeed, its very open-endedness and randomness disturbed conservative and religious opinion almost as much as the newfound commonality with the apes. For history was now potentially meaningless. Pragmatist philosophers such as John Dewey found this lack of destiny liberating, but the general response was to recast and domesticate "Darwinism." One way, natural theology aside, was to smuggle back into evolutionism older notions of heritable "acquired characteristics." This is the idea that if I exercise my biceps, my progeny will have bigger biceps too. By keeping fit and acquiring new skills, I will thus be able to promote progressive evolution, continuous improvement of race; and by maintaining healthy social conditions, society will continue its upward development along the evolutionary scale. Sloth and bad habits, alternatively, spell biological and social degeneration. Among the most fervent advocates of this view was Theodore Roosevelt.

The idea had the double advantage of putting purpose back into history and making it subject to human agency, conscious direction, *choice and responsibility*. Environment and humans alike became alterable by purposeful action. Laissez-faire was one possible political option, a system that would help the poor (and the cause of evolution) by not helping them. But these same sociobiological arguments could also be used to favor interventionism, improvement in the disagreeable conditions of the lowly and deficient. Eventually, however, after decisive advances in genetics, such "elevationism" also came to include projects of eugenics, the putatively rational control of reproduction for the purpose of improving the race. It was in that spirit, for example, that several American states passed sterilization measures in the early part of this century.

Biological theories, then, could be deployed to support a whole range of political positions. Evolutionary links between humans and animals could be invoked to emphasize that the junglelike realities of society, "the struggle for existence," were inscribed in our very nature. The ecological elements of Darwinism could be used, on the other hand, to emphasize interdependence and the need for cooperation. On balance, however, the chief function of these theories was to reinforce the pleasing idea that existing hierarchies, racial and social, were "natural" and no doubt destined to be reinforced on a global scale tomorrow.

John Burgess, founder of political science at Columbia University and Theodore Roosevelt's law teacher, was more inclined to Hegelian state theory and the inevitable, providentially ordained rise of the nation-state under the aegis of various branches of the "Teutonic" race. What is especially noteworthy about Burgess is his analysis of civilized right. Contrary to the eighteenth-century doctrines of universal rights expressed, for example, in the Declaration of Independence, Burgess insisted that pre-political barbarism had no intrinsic rights whatsoever in relation to the Teutonic nations. "The civilized states," he maintained, "have a claim upon the uncivilized populations, as well as a duty towards them, and that claim is that they shall become civilized." Failing to achieve civilization on their own, they would have "to submit to the powers that can do it for them." There would have to be a clearance operation to make way for "the abode of civilized man." Hence the "transcendent right and duty to establish political and legal order everywhere" also entailed "a great world-duty" for the civilized nations to eradicate "permanent instability on the part of any state or semi-state" on the periphery. In principle, then, there was a right and obligation to intervene whenever and wherever the Teutons saw fit.

Alfred T. Mahan, the final figure of our foursome, was the only American intellectual of the epoch to gain extensive international stature. A captain in the navy, he was mediocre at sea; but on land, at the Naval War College, he turned into the preeminent intellectual of global navalism. His book *The Influence of Sea Power upon History* (1890) became the canonical reference work for the growing naval world community, providing ample historical justification for the vigorous expansion of navies that was already under way. The German Kaiser was a devoted reader, and Queen Victoria invited Mahan for a chat. He and his friends Theodore Roosevelt and Henry Cabot Lodge (the Massachussetts senator) constituted a well-connected naval pressure group in the 1890s. Roosevelt's interest, especially, was of long standing. His very first book, written at the advanced age of twenty-one, had been entitled *The Naval War of 1812* (1879).

The rise of Great Britain formed the centerpiece of Mahan's historical reflection. A combination of geographic insularity and gradually growing control over strategic seaways had made the

British a hegemonic power. From this he deduced trans-historical lessons about the nature of geopolitical power and, above all, the relatively superior value of sea power (thus demonstrating little understanding of either the potential impact of technological change or the historical peculiarity of the British example). As regards the United States, Mahan lamented that public and polity alike were ignoring the conflictual nature of the world and the military preparedness this required. The luxury of undisturbed expansion was rapidly coming to an end. Facing two oceans, the United States would have to build an isthmian canal, and once in place that waterway would decisively enhance the commercial and strategic value of the region around it and so attract the interest of other powers. The Caribbean was destined to become the new maritime hub, the new Mediterranean of the world. Yet the nation was pathetically unprepared mentally and materially for the urgency of projecting regional hegemony outward into the two oceans. Minimally, one would have to secure the entry lanes to the future canal. (No such foreign interest ever developed after the Panama Canal was built. The Caribbean remained on the whole an American backwater.)

Meanwhile, the world was getting smaller and living space diminishing. "Civilized man" was thus showing "aggressive restlessness," as evidenced by the growing Western desire to resume joint colonization of the barbaric world. Here, again, the United States seemed to have forgotten its ties with Western civilization. The American political machinery was unsuited for trans-oceanic expansion; and the easy life at home threatened to overtake that basic martial spirit, that "temper of stern purpose and strenuous emulation," that invigorating nationalism so necessary in the struggle for civilization abroad and against deadening, leveling socialism at home. "Merely utilitarian arguments," as Mahan put it, "have never convinced nor converted mankind." People would never "be commanded by peace, presented as the tutelary deity of the stock-market." Better, then, to join the "great mission" of the West, the vital battle to control and remake the older Asian civilizations.

Seen as a whole, then, Mahan's argument had two main aspects: first, a geopolitical theme of strategic preparedness and naval armament in an expanded theater of purely U.S. interests, directed against other Western powers (though, by virtue of affinity and necessity, in close cooperation with Britain); and, second, a civilizational discourse of conquest and uplifting. Cutting across both, however, was a deep *anxiety* about materialistic degeneration and loss of virtue, a profound sense of foreboding about the advent of mass society. To that extent, there was also doubt about inevitable progress. Discontent with civilization and cultural pessimism was of course not uncommon among the Western intelligentsia of the late nineteenth century. In the United States it touched especially some members of the older, eastern elite, who worried about being swamped by pullulating masses of lowly immigrants and feared that their own "race" and class were becoming dangerously comfortable, even losing the capacity to reproduce. Roosevelt shared the sentiment, famously denouncing the "life of slothful ease" and idealizing "the hard fighting virtues" that he deemed typical for "all the great masterful races." He himself had indeed gone west to find the properly "strenuous life." So, too, had his fellow Harvard alumnus Owen Wister. Wister was a writer from Philadelphia who was obsessed with the West, which he romanticized in a series of popular works. Like Roosevelt he was also a member of the nostalgic Boone and Crockett Club. For Wister the East was a fallen world, "debased and mongrel with its hordes of encroaching alien vermin"; whereas survival "in the clean cattle country," a space thankfully pretty free of "Poles or Huns or Russian Jews," required a "spirit of adventure, courage, and self-sufficiency."

One can see how this attitude could easily translate into a philosophy of superiority and militarism. Roosevelt's rhetoric periodically lapsed into it. One can see, too, how it coalesced with the regenerative concept of imperial expansion. Conquest here is *dual*: an internal conquest of the self, a regeneration, as well as an outward charge to purge and uplift the conquered spaces and peoples themselves. This fortifying conquest of the self is perhaps the deeper, utopian meaning of Roosevelt's cathartic experience on San Juan Hill, where the rough-riding new colonel, after many tribulations, finally had the opportunity of charging forth and shooting a Spaniard.

(5)

Seward might have found Mahan's (not to mention Roosevelt's) thinking rather crude, but the level of conceptualization had generally risen since O'Sullivan's days. The destinarian frame had been enlarged. There was more variety in the arguements, partly for the simple reason that destiny, its spatial and ethical *manifestness*, was no longer as patent. Yet notions of American "originality" and difference had to be preserved. The most immediate problem had to do with the kind of territories under consideration. Situated in some cases thousands of miles away and populated by large numbers of people not easily imagined as future Americans, these places were recognized from the beginning as inescapably different. A classification had to be found for nearly perpetual inferiority, and thus the delicate subject of colonialism was raised. I have recast the arguments, for reasons of economy as well as clarity, into a series of conceptual *clusters*, partly overlapping and suggestive of a certain imperial coherence.*

Duty and Uplifting

Once the future of the territories had to be settled, no single theme so dominated the debate as that of "duty." It sparked one of McKinley's very few pithy formulations: "Duty determines destiny." What the alliterative slogan actually was supposed to mean was typically not clear. But duty was a useful device to fall back on when the operative scope of destiny appeared a bit hazy. Doing the right thing now would work to fulfill destiny or the providential design. "I do not prophesy," McKinley confessed, for "the present is all-absorbing to me." This was not unnatural for a devout Methodist and a man of his personality; and a persistent thread of uncertainty and fear of decision runs through his pronouncements. A certain shift in causal emphasis to the present was thus taking place. Few, however, went as far as the oppositional Bryan, when he responded to McKinley by arguing that "purpose" determines destiny, a purpose that one then could de-

---

* The quotes are typical of a wide body of opinion and thus not always identified.

cide oneself. This was to suspend altogether the notion of a pre-determined and determining destiny and turn it into its opposite: pure voluntarism.

That "duty," in particular, would be the answer to uncertainty had to do with the need to put the act of ruling alien peoples without their consent in the best possible light. Rudyard Kipling's poem "White Man's Burden" expressed this theme of obligation most dramatically and famously. The Englishman wrote it explicitly in order to urge Americans to take on the "burdens" of civilization in the Philippines. Lots of Americans agreed with him, as evidenced here:

> What America wants is not territorial expansion, but expansion of civilization. We want, not to acquire the Philippines for ourselves, but to give the Philippines free schools, a free church, open courts, no caste, equal rights to all. This is for our interest.

To do one's duty is plainly to do right, so duty was hard to oppose in the abstract. Its concrete meaning, however, moved from the original identification and solidarity with the Cubans, considered an oppressed colonial people in need of democratic assistance, to a sense of superiority toward childlike wards in need of instruction (after order had forcefully been restored). To these wards in waiting was also imputed an intrinsic human right to be "rescued" from their barbarism. It was incumbent upon the civilizer to rescue them even though this might involve conquest. For if, as in the Philippines, they refused such help, only the imposition of order would allow proper fulfillment of duty. Nothing could be more negligent than leaving them in anarchy, "prey to warring factions of barbarians," as one observer said. And by fulfilling one's duty to Christianity and civilization one would actually also profit, for "with the obligations are associated recompense in the wide field of commercial development."

Race

The concept of race was all-pervasive and underpinned by the expansion of scientific (and pseudoscientific) discourse. It could signify everything from a particular linguistic group to the whole of humanity; but on the whole it was an essentialist category used to describe the inherent traits of a given group, especially "Anglo-Saxons," from whom most good things were thought to emanate: "In everything which makes a people great, the supremacy of the Anglo-American is the most prominent factor of this age." The same race instinct that had carried the Aryans out of Central Asia (alternatively, the Anglo-Saxons out of the German forests) was now carrying their American descendants outward toward the Pacific, namely, "the racial aspiration to be a great nation."

This aspiration, then, had to be obeyed. Speaking on the annexation of Hawaii in 1898, for example, Representative Charles F. Cochran of Missouri extolled it as "only another step in the onward march of liberty and civilization" and "the conquest of the world by the Aryan races." Triumphantly, to House applause, he added that the "reign of the Aryan, with justice, enlightenment, and the establishment of liberty, shall penetrate to every nook of the habitable globe." For "the onward march of the indomitable race that founded this Republic" could not be stopped; it was "the race which sooner or later will place the imprint of its genius and the stamp of its conscience upon civilizations everywhere."

Other races, conversely, were either dangerous or unfit. To the former belonged the vigorous Slavs, with whom was anticipated a future showdown. To the latter, recessive category belonged virtually every non-European group (and often Europeans of "Latin" origin). American blacks were largely categorized as alien. Senator John Proctor of Vermont, whose speech to the Senate about the dreadful human conditions in Cuba had convinced many to go to war, issued this telling warning when hostilities had ceased:

Let us avoid the criminal blunder made in the past, when we bestowed with unthinking liberality the highest privilege of

Anglo-Saxon freedom upon an illiterate, alien race just emerging from bondage—a priceless privilege which our fathers attained only through centuries of patient self-development—and thus prevented the placing of the rights of suffrage upon an educational basis applicable to whites and blacks alike.

Here, then, the ever-wider race laws being instituted at the state level against blacks (the domestic "wards") found a logical connection to the need to keep subject aliens abroad in their proper place.

Territorial Identity and Empire

Thorny issues attached to the novelty of taking charge of extracontinental territories. First, it looked remarkably like European colonialism or imperialism, which was not an idea easily digested in a former colony. Imperialism, as McKinley solemnly declared, was "foreign to the temper and genius of this free and generous people"; in short, "alien to American sentiment, thought and purpose." Attempts were made, therefore, to call it something else: empire of peace, empire of love, empire of the intellect, empire of liberty, and other poetic recodings. Another, related strategy was to distingush between the enlightened colonialism of the British and all other forms, which were based on force. As shown in India and elsewhere, the British had "already brought to a wonderful perfection" the kind of "democratic empire" that the Americans were now "destined to create." Thus, as fellow Anglo-Saxons and future "co-workers in the tasks of civilization," Americans would emulate the English and turn colonialism into *tutelage*, preparation for republican self-government at some suitable future date. One could even call it a "New Imperialism," since it was "destined to carry world-wide the principles of Anglo-Saxon peace and justice, liberty and law."

When colonial administration actually began, observers were therefore at some considerable pains to distinguish American rule from the preceding Spanish. This was not always easy. In the

Philippines, for example, the U.S. forces found it useful to copy the Spanish policy of *reconcentrados*—removing peasants to strategic hamlets (to use a term from a more recent war), the very policy that earlier in Cuba had caused humanitarian outrage in the United States and been an important reason to go to war. But the similarity was only apparent:

> The United States and Spain have both shut their reconcentrados in reservations; but there the analogy ends. Spain has starved hers; the United States has spent millions of dollars in feeding hers. Spain has refused hers all access to civilization and all preparation for liberty; the United States has expended millions of dollars yearly in schools to educate hers and to prepare them for citizenship in a Free Republic. . . .

There were those, however, who did not flinch from embracing colonialism pure and simple. They thought it was a good thing and not at all incompatible with democracy at home. That a nation presumably based on the idea that "all men are created equal" would now rule subject populations was not a conceptual difficulty. Once understood as wards or children, they could be classed with such excluded domestic groups as women, blacks, and Indians. And here, readily available, was indeed a long domestic experience to draw upon, namely, that of handling subject populations of Indians. The question throughout the nineteenth century had been how to classify them: Were they inside or outside the United States? The interesting answer, in due course, was: Neither. For their status as independent nations underwent gradual diminution, yet never permitted inclusion and citizenship. Once defined in 1831 as "domestic, dependent nations," they could be governed as subjects and not citizens. By the late nineteenth century, their legal position had been readjusted downward to that of local dependent communities in need of protective control, tutelage, and direction, to be provided by the Federal Bureau of Indian Affairs, which indeed ruled supreme.

This uplifting example, then, was most useful because it made it easier to conceptualize aliens as well as territories that were supposed to be both inside and outside the United States. Hitherto territorial status had been a *stage* preparatory to statehood, though admittedly New Mexico had to wait a long time on account of its population. But it was spatially and culturally difficult to imagine that the Philippines, thousands of miles away with a population of millions, would ever become a state; even the most supremacist thinkers had a hard time anticipating when this racially mixed population would recede or disappear. Thus Puerto Rico and the Philippines ingeniously ended up being both outside and inside, Cuba became nominally independent, while Hawaii, alien majorities notwithstanding, did become a state half a century later.

The new heterogeneity was reflected inversely in the nearly universal conviction that the Spanish-American War had laid to rest the remaining wounds from the Civil War and so forever sealed the unity and homogeneity of the *continental* Union.

Geographic Determinism

Admiral Dewey's startling victory in Manila Bay sent McKinley to a map he had ripped out of an old geography book, and thus, like numberless others, he began to reimagine the character of that map. Hawaii now looked even more like a providentially designed halfway station in the middle of the Pacific. Perhaps the Philippines had in fact been thrust into American hands to complete the series of stepping-stones to Asia. This "highway" of the ocean fit the expectation that the Pacific was destined to be the new commercial space par excellence. And one could then recast all of the above in terms of the westward course of empire, or the instinctual return to the Aryan cradle. Indeed, new maps were produced that showed Honolulu as the communication center of a wholly new Pacific world.

Nevertheless, a break with the contiguity principle had undeniably taken place. Manifest destiny, it turned out, had ceased to be predetermined continentalism. The Philippines presented a particular problem in that they were spatially a part of the Old World, the dichotomous Other of the "New." How was one to square this with the consecrated Monroe Doctrine? That cornerstone of U.S. foreign relations was after all premised on the distinction between the New and the Old Worlds, between which there was to be no mutual interference. Seizing the islands, therefore, would make the United States part and parcel of the Old World and probably entangle the nation in some Old-style business. But this sticky point was either evaded by rhetorical claims to the effect that the spirit of generosity expressed in the Monroe Doctrine vis-à-vis Latin America was now merely being extended; or it was peremptorily dismissed.

The Disease of Isolation

One way of doing that was simply to declare the advent of a new stage, now that the nation had finally matured and left isolation behind. John Ireland, a Catholic archbishop, put it well in the fall of 1898:

> To-day we proclaim a new order of things. America is too great to be isolated from the world around her and beyond her. She is a world-power, to whom no world-interest is alien, whose voice reaches afar, whose spirit travels across seas and mountain ranges to most distinct continents and islands; and with America goes far and wide what America in her grandest ideal represents—democray and liberty, a government of the people, by the people, for the people. This is Americanism, more than American territory, or American shipping, or American soldiery. Where this grandest ideal of American life is not held supreme, America has not reached; where this ideal is supreme, America reigns.

Catholics otherwise tended to be less gung ho about attacks on Catholic nations in the name of Protestant Anglo-Saxonism; but the equation of Americanism with a "new order of things" and with universal liberty and democracy is familiar by now. What is noteworthy instead is the idea that greatness is incompatible with isolation. Typically, this was then connected up with a humanitarian subtheme that isolation had been *selfish*. "We cannot, like

a hermit nation, shrink and shrivel into a lonely and selfish isolation," one observer said. A sort of morbid introspection was implied, unhealthy, even narcissistic preoccupation with oneself
(hinting perhaps at more unspeakable practices).

Not for the last time, there was thus an erroneous conviction
that, "once and for all," the United States had entered the world
at large. The nation would assume proper responsibility for world
affairs. This was an illusion shared by several foreign chancelleries.

Commercial Vistas

Commerce figured throughout. One would have been surprised
had it not. Commerce, together with Christianity, was after all
supposed to be the outstanding civilizer. And Dewey's victory had
made business interests, at long last, perk up with enthusiasm.
Fantasies of marvelous future markets in the Far East proliferated. Little commerce actually materialized. Otherwise, in the
larger frame of international relations, commerce was understood
in polar contrast either to promote peace or to increase friction
and conflict. From each perspective, however, one could argue
that territorial expansion in the Pacific was an altogether excellent
thing. A great deal of hyperbole was uttered here: mastering the
Pacific would be the beginning of mastering the future of global
commerce and so on. References to plain profitability were perhaps more common. Few could rival in this regard the lucidity of
Whitelaw Reid, a newspaperman who had been Republican candidate for Vice President in 1892 and peace negotiator with Spain
in 1898. Denouncing "mushy sentimentality," he brushed aside
any objections to retaining the Philippines:

Planted directly in front of the Chinese colossus, on a great
territory of our own, we have the first and best chance to
profit by his awakening. Commanding both sides of the Pacific, and the available coal supplies on each, we command
the ocean that, according to the old prediction, is to bear the
bulk of the world's commerce in the twentieth century.

Thus (in a Jacksonian phrase) the "extension of ordered liberty" into one of "the dark places of the earth" would bring benefits to everyone, not only to Americans but to "our new wards" and "to mankind." Commerce was a precise measure of civilization.

Evangelization

The other side of the commercializing mission, then, was the Christianization of the world. This was very much conceived as conquest. In the words of a key figure: "The Christian religion is inherently expansive, and the idea of a world-wide conquest entered its heart and brain from the very beginning." *The Outlook*, Theodore Roosevelt's favorite Christian magazine (circulation over 100,000), concurred:

> We have no right to abandon some part of the world, and say, That belongs to the world; we will leave it alone. The function of the Christian Church is to take the world and the whole world, all material things and all activities, and consecrate them to service of God, and thus make them serve God because they serve humanity.

Much of the talk about mission and destiny remained explicitly Christian, and Christian professionals, as the great example of Josiah Strong had demonstrated, were generally much in favor of expansion for this reason. Yet the arguments of the 1890s, just like the world, had extended beyond purely Christian concerns. In fact, it had become possible to think of these precisely *as* Christian concerns, pervading everything in principle and so a fundamental given but in actual life one thing or activity among others. Christianity, then, was a sort of umbrella covering a range of other arguments, but it was not as pervasively and immediately present as it was in the 1840s.

Realpolitik

Few celebrants of the end of isolation advocated any descent into European-style power politics. The United States would bring to bear its essential qualities, the most advanced extant, in the civilizational and commercial uplifting of the world. A small but important group went further. Mahan has already been discussed. Henry Cabot Lodge, though often lcw-key because of vocal anti-imperialism within Boston's establishment, espoused the sort of economic geopolitics that was now common in European thinking:

> The great nations of the earth are competing in a desperate struggle for the world's trade, and in that competition . . . we must not be left behind. In the economic struggle the great nations of Europe for many years have been seizing all the waste places, and all the weakly held lands of the earth, as the surest means of trade development.

He was convinced that South America would have been partitioned like Africa if the United States had not prevented it. But for Lodge military jockeying for commercial advantage was not a mere cyclical game. In this new epoch small was being eaten by big and the United States could not stay aloof from such a lethal development. "For the unfit among nations," he said, "there is no pity in the relentless world-forces which shape the destinies of mankind." Hence the need for military preparedness and prudent expansion. Peering at the Russians in Asia, he foresaw the moment when Anglo civilization would one day have to confront "a power controlling an extent of territory and a mass of population the like of which the world has never seen." This "colossus of despotism and military socialism" would indeed endanger "the welfare of every free people." Lodge was of course referring here to tsarist Russia, not the Soviet Union.

In this vision he was by no means alone. His friend Brooks Adams presented the fullest form of it in a series of works of immense historical sweep, pointing to a grand future struggle with the Eastern empire. Others, less ambitiously, simply referred to the Russian "race" as "the most inimical to every element of Anglo-American civilization; differing from us in language, literature, religion, and government, and vigorously antagonistic to all our conceptions of human rights and human duties." Japan, a few years later, would radically shake this view of Russia as the main threat. By trouncing the Russians militarily in 1905, the Japanese reinforced the incipient suspicion on the part of some geopolitical savants that the Philippines were really a strategic liability. Mahan, to his credit, had always been skeptical.

History and Civilization

It was agreed that civilization would conquer barbarism and that the United States would (if acting rightly) become a powerful presence and model on the world stage in its capacity as the most advanced form of civilization anywhere. All things being equal, the end of history was American democracy as enshrined in the trinity "free government, free commerce, and free men." Apprehension concerned only the political will to carry out one's responsibilities and the ability to do it right. Time was also accelerating and space diminishing, making the world faster and smaller. Failing to keep up when only the fittest survived meant degeneracy and doom. Witness the opulent, effete, isolationist China, sunk in Oriental stagnation and corruption, incapable of presenting a dignified appearance to the world. It was essential, therefore, always *to be on the move.* Spatial stagnation meant regression. Destiny required constant, purposeful intervention in time and space.

(6)

Senator Albert J. Beveridge of Indiana, after Roosevelt the most charismatic young Republican, will provide a suitable bridge here to our next section on anti-imperialism. No one expressed so eloquently and unabashedly the imperialist position in toto. His views, though suffused to an unusual degree with Christian rhetoric, form a graphic summary of the preceding themes and thus a good contrast to the following part. Beveridge, it should be borne in mind, was a Progressive reformer through and through, favoring such typical reforms as meat inspection, regulation of railways, antitrust measures, and the eight-hour day. In 1912, he left the Republicans to join Roosevelt's Progressive Party.

Like Roosevelt, Beveridge was much concerned early on about the decline in the quality of the American citizenry, which he thought was losing its basic Puritan elements. Material wealth, especially, was undermining the desire for "nobler ideals and braver action." Like Roosevelt, too, he invented a political identity by distancing himself from the narrow class interests of capital and labor alike. Unlike the elitist New Yorker, however, Beveridge maintained a religious faith in "the plain people of the Republic," whom he took to be "the voice of God" and therefore, in the abstract, always right.

Soon afterward, luckily, the Spanish-American War created room for bracing, noble action in ample measure for "His chosen people." On the eve of it, Beveridge chose to recall (quite unfairly) the example of Ulysses Grant:

> He never forgot that we are a conquering race and that we must obey our blood and occupy new markets, and, if necessary, new lands. He had the prophet's seer-like sight which beheld, as a part of the Almighty's infinite plan, the disappearance of debased civilizations and decaying races before the higher civilization of the nobler and more virile types of man. . . . He had the instinct of empire.

It was this inherent, racial instinct that had made Americans and Anglophones "the exploring, the colonizing, the administrating force of the world." Empire now meant increasing commerce and colonial power and the United States was rightfully joining:

> We shall establish trading-posts throughout the world as distributing points for American products. We shall cover the oceans with our merchant marine. We shall build a navy to the measure of our greatness. Great colonies, flying our flag and trading with us, will grow about our posts of trade. Our

institutions will follow our flag on the wings of our commerce. And American law, American order, American civilization and the American flag will plant themselves on shores, hitherto bloody and benighted, but, by those agencies of God, henceforth to be made beautiful and bright.

Opponents of this destiny he deemed "apostates," unable to read "divinely logical" history properly. "Events," he argued, "are the arguments of God" and "we are the allies of events," which is to say "the ceaseless march of free institutions." Free, alas, did not necessarily signify the right to consent for everyone, but *by definition* American sovereignty could be "nothing but a blessing to any people and to any land." As he asked rhetorically, "would not the people of the Philippines prefer the just, humane, civilizing government of this Republic to the savage, bloody rule of pillage and extortion from which we have rescued them?" Hence, then, the obvious need for order:

Rebellion against the authority of the flag must be crushed without delay, for hesitation encourages revolt; and without anger, for the turbulent children know not what they do. And then civilization must be organized, administered, and maintained. Law and justice must rule where savagery, tyranny, and caprice have rioted. The people must be taught the art of orderly and continuous industry.

The whole of history was in a sense just a predestined rescue operation, rescuing the world "from its natural wilderness and from savage men," an inevitable, evolutionary process by which the world was subjected to order and liberty. This act of subjection Beveridge imagined very vividly, as in the following flourish of near psychosexual violence:

A hundred wildernesses are to be subdued. Unpenetrated regions must be explored. Unviolated valleys must be tilled. Unmastered forests must be felled. Unriven mountains must be torn asunder and their riches of gold and iron and ores of price must be delivered to the world.

All, then, for the good purpose of achieving "commercial supremacy," which itself would serve to make the United States "the
sovereign factor in the peace of the world." Thus he envisioned
that "nations shall war no more without the consent of the American Republic." God had indeed appointed Americans (and, to a
lesser extent, other Anglophones) "lords of civilization" or "the
master organizers of the world," so that they would "establish
system where chaos reigns." In the end, the world would be "regenerated" and universal peace begin under American auspices.

(7)

In 1893, when the annexation of Hawaii was initially on the
agenda, Carl Schurz wrote a stinging attack in *Harper's Magazine*
on the whole idea of manifest destiny. It surfaces, he noted, in
every annexationist moment to make opposition seem like "a
struggle against fate." Thus it disguised the real interests behind
expansion. Schurz was not against expansion as such; he supported a consensual union with the roughly similar Canada. Such
a homogeneous entity would make sense politically and, because
of its continentalist logic, would not lead to any further aggrandizement. To the south, on the contrary, there was no such logical
end to expansion, and the populations were heterogeneous. The
tropics were not conducive to democracy anyway. Annexations in
the Caribbean and Pacific would only undermine a uniquely favorable situation:

> We are the only one that is not in any of its parts threatened
> by powerful neighbors; the only one not under any necessity
> of keeping up a large armament either on land or water for
> the security of its possessions; the only one that can turn all
> the energies of its population to productive employment; the
> only one that has an entirely free hand.

Why, he asked, willingly create vulnerabilities? It would circumscribe one's range of action instead of opening it up. Hence there
was no need either for any bloated navy. A sensible policy was
instead to secure through negotiation rights to certain coaling sta-

tions and sources of raw materials, while concentrating on developing "the exceptional and invaluable advantages" already at hand within.

Schurz, originally a political émigré from the German revolt of 1848, rose in Republican politics to become Secretary of the Interior under Hayes in the late 1870s. His position on expansionism had remained the same since he opposed the annexation of Santo Domingo in 1870. He presented it in the form of a bind: the United States, in order to preserve its basic nature, could not take in territories as dominions but only as full members-to-be; but if one did bring such alien spaces and populations in as full members, the essential character of the country would change anyway. The self-evident conclusion was to refrain.

Opposition to destinarian expansion was wider in both scope and dissemination than in the 1840s. It encompassed, for example, a radical socialist critique far outside the mainstream that categorized the whole enterprise as capitalist robbery pure and simple. Since the main interest here, however, is to reveal the destinarian limits of the mainstream itself, I shall leave radicals generally to the side. Many within the opposition were of eminently established background: former President Grover Cleveland, Republican Speaker of the House Thomas Reed, Massachusetts Senator Hoar (member of the so-called Republican Old Guard), Andrew Carnegie, David Starr Jordan (president of Stanford) and many other educators, relatively fewer ministers. William Jennings Bryan was opposed, of course, as was indeed former Republican President Benjamin Harrison, though he chose to say little. How far and how wide the criticality stretched was an individual matter. I shall summarize the arguments, in ascending order of importance, under three general rubrics:

Empirical Disagreements

By this I mean differences about facts or factual probabilities without any necessary disagreement about the discursive frame as such.

Thus it was argued that no commercial bonanza was likely in

the Far East; that the climate made it impossible for Anglo-Saxons to sustain real colonization; that superior Anglo-Saxons were more likely to be degraded by contact with inferiors rather than the latter being uplifted; that the Filipinos, while not perhaps as capable as Anglo-Saxons, were able to take care of themselves; that, in any case, Americans had a very bad record taking care of "wards" domestically, as evidenced by blacks and Indians; that there could be no duty to civilize Filipinos as they were not actually under the control of the United States anyway but had to be subjugated; that it was a silly idea to kill people one was presumably trying to lift up; that the various new possessions, especially the Philippines, were strategic traps rather than assets; that the United States had no bureaucratic machinery to deal with colonial peoples and was hopelessly inept at great-power diplomacy, both of which would now be necessary; that imperialism in the sense of political control was old hat and inferior to purely commercial relations; that continental, contiguous expansion before 1898 was qualitatively different from imperialism; that the United States had plenty of territory it needed to develop and problems to tackle before venturing out into the transoceanic sphere.

Many of these points were sound.

The Fate of American Identity

Expansion engendered a deeper controversy about "our place and work in the world" and "what we wish our America to become," as one critic succinctly put the matter. "We must remain a peculiar people" was one rather desperate response. On the subject of remaining peculiar, the opposition argued in a variety of ways that a colonial or imperial career would ruin the essential nature of the country or at least throw it into crisis. Schurz's paradox encapsulates this view. Races and spaces alien in every sense could not be incorporated, but if they were excluded, the shameful two-class system that the Civil War had been fought to do away with would reappear. Republics could not have subject populations and stay healthy: they had to be homogeneous. Furthermore, colonialism would infect and degrade the consciousness and culture of the colonizer. Virtue and honest citizenship would be endangered. For the first time, very likely, there would be standing armies and a tendency to militarism, followed by taxes. Other traditions such as nonentanglement in European politics would also be declared null and void. The United States, in sum, would fall into the world and cease to be itself.

This did not happen. The nation did not, for better or worse, finally "fall into the world" until half a century later through World War II and the cold war; and even then not the whole way. None of the colonial or semicolonial moves had any fundamental effect on the historical trajectory of continental United States or on its identity in the world; and when this became increasingly clear after 1900, the anti-imperialist cause foundered. What proponents and opponents alike had imagined as an epochal change turned out to be, if not an "aberration," considerably less than decisive. Some anti-imperialists such as Charles Francis Adams, Jr., were in fact careful not to exaggerate the potential structural effects and emphasized instead the inconsistencies and errors of the reigning views.

Critique of Manifest Destiny

As the example of Schurz indicates, there was also a direct, if not very common, assault on the whole notion of destiny, providential or historical. Senator Pettigrew issued one such indictment in 1898 during the debate over Hawaii:

> Throughout all recorded time manifest destiny has been the murderer of men. It has committed more crimes, done more to oppress and wrong the inhabitants of the world than any other tribute to which mankind has fallen heir. Manifest destiny has caused the strong to rob the weak and has reduced the weak to slavery. Manifesty destiny built the feudal castle and supplied the castle with its serfs. Manifest destiny impelled republics that have heretofore existed and perished to go forth and conquer weaker races and to subject their people

to slavery, to impose taxation against their will, and to inflict governments odious to them. Manifest destiny is simply the cry of the strong in justification of their plunder of the weak.

E. L. Godkin, editor of *The Nation*, in which he wrote sarcastic pieces against the pretensions of "the firm Duty & Destiny," emphasized that it was really "one set of human wills against another set, and our destiny will be whatever is determined by the more powerful set." If duty determines destiny, who determines duty? he asked pointedly. Godkin was a conservative, crudely antilabor and dismissive of the new immigrants. Yet he was also among those—Senator Hoar was another—who related the hypocritical talk of "saving" aliens abroad to the continuing lynchings of blacks at home and to the emerging state laws against their right to mobility. "We do not have to go to Luzon [in the Philippines] for American barbarities," a Unitarian preacher in Brooklyn noted and went on to mention that an excursion train from Atlanta had been organized to witness the latest lynching in Georgia.

In condensing the oppositional view, I have made it more cohesive than it really was. Throughout one tended to come up against a basic contradiction, on which indeed the expansionists came down gleefully again and again: the United States had always been about subjugation and displacement, thus demonstrating, as Henry Cabot Lodge proudly declared, "a record of conquest, colonization, and territorial expansion unequalled by any people in the nineteenth century." If no more territory could be taken because it was contrary to essential American principles, one might as well give New Mexico back to the Apaches. Against this forceful point, the contiguity argument seemed quite lame.

(8)

The Apache example came from Theodore Roosevelt, and the moment has now come to return to this extraordinary figure, whom fortuitous (and tragic) circumstances put into the White House in 1901. His ascendancy had not appeared likely. When he became governor of New York after the highly visible heroics on San Juan Hill, Godkin said of him superciliously, if not inaccurately, that he would have made a good pal of Richard the Lion-hearted, for his outlook was "essentially a boy's view." Less accurately, Godkin went on to predict that if this view were ever turned into "national policy" the result "would make us the most turbulent people the world has ever seen." But, Godkin was happy to observe, only Roosevelt himself took his histrionics of war seriously.

There was indeed a good deal of Rooseveltian blustering about the need to become a great virile power. "We cannot, if we would, play the part of China, and be content to rot by inches in ignoble ease within our borders, taking no interest in what goes on beyond them, sunk in a scrambling commercialism; heedless of the higher life, the life of aspiration, of toil and risk," to quote a typical passage from 1899. Destiny he interpreted, very much in charac-ter, in voluntaristic terms. One had the choice of determining it with one's own hands, so to speak; it was up to each to show the will, desire, and decisiveness to act in accordance with one's his-torical duty. And that duty, in the American case, was now to be Great.

In office, Roosevelt actually performed on the whole with con-summate skill and prudence in the foreign arena. He knew more about it and had greater intuitive feel for it than any U.S. Presi-dent since John Quincy Adams. Unlike Woodrow Wilson, he was a superb tactician, with a nuanced grasp of threats, force, ap-pearances, dissimulation, retreat, the whole technology of power politics. Yet Roosevelt's presidency was in fact marked by the growing domestic agenda of Progressivism and his moves to es-tablish the Executive domestically as a relatively autonomous, policy-making institution. His geopolitical maneuvers, often out of sight of the public, were made with keen appreciation of how limited was the American willingness to enter into the high-stakes game of global politics, a game in which he himself took the greatest interest. Within a determinate range of geopolitics, he enjoyed complete privacy and freedom of action; but the range itself was not wide. The United States was now perceived by oth-ers as a Great Power, however, and Roosevelt consciously played his role when he could as though he were heading one. I bring him in here because of his articulate intelligence on the matter and the endlessly fascinating (and often-made) contrast with Woodrow Wilson, the exploration of which reveals something about the destiny of destinarian thinking after 1900.

Roosevelt's strategic approach has usefully been characterized as domination in the Caribbean, balance of power in the Far East, and nonentanglement in Europe, coupled with adjudication in Great Power conflicts when possible for the purpose of promoting civilized peace. The particulars of this are not my concern here; the interest lies in his long-term project of civilization and geopolitics, the place of the United States within it, and how it all changed. Let us begin with his historical understanding of time and space.

History appeared to Roosevelt as a linear movement from barbarism to civilization but through an intermediate or transitional stage of despotism. We recognize this view as essentially Spencer's, but Roosevelt used it spatially to divide the real world of 1900 in two: a sphere of civilization (Christian, Western civilization, the Anglophone version being the cutting edge) against a sphere of barbarism and despotism, civilization of course gradually expanding. Empire as civilized domination showed the historical necessity of establishing order by means of force in the unruly sphere and thus allowing "waste spaces" to be used in the interest of humanity. American history, in a way, was the story of just such a process. A certain amount of cruelty and brutality necessarily adhered to the endeavor, and it was useless, therefore, to moralize about that past. The result was in any case for the best. Putting down the Philippine "insurrection" was thus the equivalent of putting down the Seminoles in Jackson's days. One must, Roosevelt advised the Secretary of State in 1899, "harass and smash the insurgents in every way until they are literally beaten into peace."

The concept of order Roosevelt had in mind signified a system of protection and obedience. The imperial power would make the rules and punish transgression but, by the same token, would also be obliged to provide protection (as well as education and welfare) and an example to emulate. This would then fill the dual function of advancing the savages toward civilization and keeping the imperial power in good trim. (Roosevelt was obsessed with fitness.)

Everyone, by definition, thus had the same interest. Yet everyone did not have to have a specifically American system. Characteristics were inherited, and societies, just like people, were different; states and nations must therefore have systems suited to them.

Within the civilized sphere, where order already reigned, it was of the essence to prevent internecine warfare and otherwise to take care of U.S. interests. To expand the cherished navy, meanwhile, was always to expand the forces of order and civilization. The decisive element for everyone everywhere was in the last analysis proper *conduct*, to be judged according to an unchanging code of civilized duty, honor, and law. A particular responsibility rested on the strong here: "Self-restraint, self-mastery, common sense, the power of accepting individual responsibility and yet of acting in conjunction with others, courage and resolution—these are the qualities which mark a masterful people."

None of this should be taken as mere rhetoric or background considerations. Roosevelt acted accordingly. The most striking illustration is his famous Corollary of 1904, modeled, I think, on the ideas of his teacher John Burgess. Officially a corollary to the Monroe Doctrine, it actually transformed what had generally been a negative injunction to keep Europeans out of Latin America into a positive right of American intervention in the Caribbean basin. The wording, as usual, was blunt:

All this country desires is to see the neighboring countries stable, orderly, and prosperous. Any country whose people conduct themselves well can count upon our heady friendship. If a nation shows that it knows how to act with reasonable efficiency and decency in social and political matters, if it keeps order and pays its obligations, it need fear no interference from the United States. Chronic wrongdoing, or an impotence which results in a general loosening of the ties of civilized society, may in America, as elsewhere, ultimately require intervention by some civilized nation, and in the Western Hemisphere the adherence of the United States to the Monroe Doctrine may force the U.S., however reluctantly, in flagrant cases of such wrongdoing or impotence, to the exercise of an international police power.

He was telling the Caribbean nations, then, something like this. As long as you behave and do not fall into irreparable internal and external disorder, we, the United States, will look upon you with benevolence. If, on the other hand, you do bad things or degenerate, we will do *whatever it takes* to keep you on the straight and narrow. As the civilizing nation in the region, we are the ones who will tell you where that path lies and when you step away from it. When you deviate, we will discipline and punish you. This is our duty and task. To do otherwise would not be proper conduct on our part.

A whole conceptual system of boundaries, transgression, quasi-legal judgment, and punishment had thus been introduced. To put it differently, the Caribbean had been declared a de facto protectorate, subject to *policing*. This is partly the sense, incidentally, in which "order," for a very brief moment, was being offered as the new American approach to the world at the time of the Gulf War. Roosevelt, at any rate, thought it an excellent model for civilized powers to follow in other geopolitical theaters. Among these powers he included Japan. He largely supported Japan when it expanded into Korea, even considering it for a while a future "regenerator of all eastern Asia." It should be understood here that once "order" had been introduced on the teleological assumption that it represented a civilizational step forward, deviance from it was automatically regression, which the civilized power of responsibility must then dutifully prevent. This kind of reasoning is identical to the Soviet Brezhnev Doctrine, used in 1968 to justify the invasion of Czechoslovakia by the Warsaw Pact forces when that country seemed to be regressing from the more advanced socialist stage into capitalism.

In 1909, when Roosevelt had left the White House and gone hunting for big game in Africa, a youngish intellectual, Herbert Croly, published a book that both synthesized and elaborated on the experience of Roosevelt's presidency. *The Promise of American Life* called for a break in tradition by means of a dynamic new nationalism of strong, purposeful government, neo-Hamiltonianism with a democratic twist. Croly's work impressed Roosevelt so much that it became the conceptual sourcebook for his gradual return to politics after 1910.

The promissory title was not chosen lightly, for Croly's book was actually a highly intelligent, sustained reflection on how one might reorient American patriotism and still retain its curious character of a religion. For Croly, this patriotism uniquely combined "loyalty to historical tradition and precedent with the imaginative projection of an ideal national Promise," a notion of a "Land of Destiny." The original democratic wager had been that a people unfettered by artificial restraints would release their energy and life would improve for everyone. Since this had worked well, said Croly, Americans had begun to think that it was a natural effect of some founding principle when it actually had more to do with historical and geographic accident. Now, for the first time, one faced real choices. The "old sense of a glorious destiny" and its "automatic fulfillment" had to be transformed into "a conscious national purpose"; that is, a rational and comprehensive policy emanating from the national government. For this one would need discipline, self-denial, regulation, and control, as individualism had gone wildly awry:

> The existing concentration of wealth and financial power in the hands of a few irresponsible men is the inevitable outcome of the chaotic individualism of our political and economic organization, while at the same time it is inimical to democracy, because it tends to erect political abuses and social inequalities into a system.

Only by not leaving things to chance and fate, then, could one restore the conditions for continuing fulfillment of the promise and the destiny. (Walter Lippmann, Croly's protégé, condensed the point a few years later in the title of his book *Drift or Mastery?*) This democratic project of regulation and control, Croly argued, had in fact already begun. First the Spanish-American War had unified and mobilized the people, then Roosevelt had come along to initiate real reform. (War could be "a useful and justifiable engine of national purpose," said Croly, laboring under the misapprehension, as did so many others, that modern wars would be short and educational.) With regard to foreign relations, he advocated no radical change in immediate policy. But he emphasized that the new nationalism would not indulge the usual American tendency to imagine "some essential incompatibility between Europeanism and Americanism," a misconception that gave "a sort of religious sanctity to the national tradition of isolation." At some point, in fact, the United States might have to tip the scales in a European conflict to promote a new democratic world order. To do otherwise would be "a species of continental provincialism and chauvinism."

Croly had thereby put into focus a tension between two competing notions of destiny, a tension that could not in fact materialize until the United States had become an industrial society wholly dominated by the logic of large-scale capital accumulation and rationalization. The older, sacred-prophetic tradition viewed the future, in principle, as determined or fixed exactly in the same sense as the events of the past: it eliminated time. Destiny in the liberal-secular conception, by contrast, was a destination to be determined through human agency on rational grounds. The future, time itself, was open but predictable, subject to instrumental control: manifest destiny, history as revealed in the utopian space of America, would be *managed destiny*. In Europe, this transition to "instrumentalism" was less difficult in conceptual terms because prophecy had been attacked frontally already by the end of the seventeenth century, as the devastating political effects of the Reformation were digested and turned into historical "lessons." Prophecy was thus gradually transformed into *prognosis*, the rational calculation of means and ends within a political field of vision determined by the pursuit of power. Absolutist regimes became the norm, and the notion of heaven descending upon earth was suspended till further notice. Napoleon's remarks to Goethe on the subject of tragedy expressed the new understanding well; the destiny of old, he said, had been replaced by politics. This administrative and political rationality could then be merged in the nineteenth century with new and more liberal-bourgeois projects. In the United States, by comparison, the sacred-prophetic impulse never waned. The language remained destinarian and messianic, as Croly was keenly aware and his book frankly recognized. The problem was how to recast it in instrumental ways.

The promotional opportunity for the United States to promote a new world order would, at any rate, arise sooner than Croly anticipated. And when it did, his hero Roosevelt and the new Progressive protagonist Wilson would both, in different ways, embrace his view.

IV

FALLING INTO THE WORLD

1914 – 1990

The First World War put a brutal end to any residual ideas of civilizational imperialism or peaceful laissez-faire capitalism without borders. The colonial moment had in fact already peaked by the time Roosevelt created the Panama Canal Zone in 1903, though it would take another half century before liberation struggles and decolonization recast domination into other forms. By 1903, too, the aging Herbert Spencer had become a disillusioned man. The rationality of capitalism had turned in unforeseen directions, developing into ever-stronger states with glittering new military machines. Strangely, international capitalism was becoming an arena of militarism and intensifying conflict among Great Powers, not at all the predicted destiny of growing interdependence, peace, and harmony.

Spencer did not live to see the ensuing denouement, the implosion and explosion of "civilization" in generalized war. From then on, the "West" could no longer be imagined in quite the same manner, nor international capitalism. This new state of affairs required, or should have required, reconsideration of the American place in the world. A serious but abortive attempt in that vein was indeed made, by Woodrow Wilson. American foreign relations ever since have been marked, one way or another, by his attempt to accomplish the dual task of bringing the United States into the world while maintaining purity and distance.

In these final remarks, therefore, I shall consider Wilson's project and then, very sketchily, follow the vicissitudes of American "destiny" during the twentieth century against that background ending with a reflection on the period after the Second World War when the United States began to think of itself as leader of the free world.

(2)

Before his presidency, Wilson had showed no signs of reforming zeal in foreign affairs. He had supported the war against Spain, but had had next to nothing to say about it or international politics generally. A single memorandum, some scattered remarks revealing nothing so much as a strong desire to be safely in the middle, an inkling that the experience of war had opened up possibilities for better national government at home: rather a meager sum total for a well-known scholar of political systems. But Wilson's orientation was actually parochial, his views those of a markedly puritanical man, stirred intellectually, it seemed, chiefly by the problems of comparative administration, like Calvin indeed a man who believed administration on behalf of the Divine (and the "people" in Wilson's case) was the Christian duty par excellence: not much there, one would have thought, by way of raw material for a world-historical figure. If anything stood out, it was his fixation on order and his stubborn belief that humankind was essentially reasonable, by which he imagined that, given the proper chance, people would always settle differences through discussion and negotiation. People (and nations) who were unreasonable and failed to abide by openly agreed rules were thus outlaws (and, by implication, sinners). This is how, later on, he came to read Bolshevism: an illegitimate minority in a disorderly, dissolved society, a "poison" and an "infection."

His historical perspective was otherwise the conventional one for a man of his background: the United States was uniquely blessed; war and revolution were bad and unhealthy; organic, orderly progress was conversely good and healthy; civilization and enlightenment, the "democratic empire," would one day rule the world; the United States, with some modifications, offered the best example, and its history was a key to understanding universal history; the civilized, meanwhile, should govern inferiors; (contradictorily) human beings are inherently good and will do the right thing if allowed their just liberty and orderly self-government; and certain individuals and nations are bound to lead because they have been privy to, or are embodiments of, the deeper providential purposes of history. Christianity was for him more than the cornerstone of civilization it appeared to be for Roosevelt; it was an always-present existential fact, pervading his language and dominating his outlook. After all, he was the son of a formidable Presbyterian minister. Wilson's messianic passages about the League of Nations read like a throwback to an earlier era of blood and redemption, the language of transcendence. He was not merely being prophetic. He was being apocalyptic in a seventeenth-century manner.

It would be overly hasty, however, to reiterate the simple contrast between Roosevelt the realist and Wilson the idealist. It illuminates little. Teddy Roosevelt would certainly have done a much better job at Versailles with the same program; Wilson, as John Maynard Keynes said afterward, was singularly "incompetent" for a statesman "in the agilities of the council chamber." Technical skill aside, though, Wilson was not averse to the brazen use of power. He intervened in Latin America, Mexico above all, far more than the imperial Roosevelt. Nor can Wilson's reform of international power politics, the "new world order" to use his term, be reduced to sheer idealism. He had hoped, in fact, that the United States would be able to dictate this program to exhausted participants at the end of the war. His millenarian rhetoric was also tempered philosophically by an admiration for the gradualist conservatism of Edmund Burke.

Yet Wilson's new world order was certainly a regenerative, liberal one, and it was to be led, in no uncertain terms, by the United States. Here he really did differ profoundly from Roosevelt, who was inclined, in Croly's neo-Hamiltonian terms, to see no "essential incompatibility" between the United States and the other powers within Western civilization. Young and vigorous, the American nation would perhaps one day become the New Rome, the latest or even last incarnation of the continuous movement of this civilization; it was not, as it would be for Wilson, a New Israel, a nation elect, messianically destined to give law and order to the world in the form of collective security. Wilson's remains the most quintessentially American attempt, the purest and most puritanical attempt, to recast international relations in the twentieth century; and this may also be the reason it is still very much with us. Our interest, then, lies in the nature of this Wilsonian liberalism with its combination of Christian destiny and collective security; and in the disputes over the meaning of "true Americanism."

The overwhelming majority view in 1914 was that the United States should stay out of the war. Wilson shared this position but was unusual in his conviction, stated forthrightly by 1916, that the international system would have to be reformed completely under American leadership afterward. Though Anglophilic, he wanted the United States to appear impeccably neutral so as to be able to play the role of the arbiter and get the belligerents to peace negotiations based on the premise of no gains. Roosevelt, on the other hand, argued (vociferously) for immediate military "preparedness" with a view to intervene. The war had rocked to the core his conception of the world. His response was to blame Germany, whose conduct against neutral, civilized Belgium he found reprehensible beyond belief. Imperial Germany had clearly regressed to the despotic stage, and the manifest duty of the United States was therefore to do all in its might to crush the Kaiser. For righteousness, as Roosevelt had once lectured Carl Schurz, always took precedence over peace. To be neutral between right and wrong was to be wrong. Above all, one was not to be *timid* in the face of wrong. Roosevelt hated timidity and so he came to hate Wilson, whom he considered the quintessence of timidity. But, then again, the Rough Rider died in early 1919, before Wilson's final, herculean crusade for the new League of Nations, a crusade that would physically cripple the President.

If Roosevelt got nowhere with the issue of military preparedness, Wilson was not successful as a neutral peacemaker. Meanwhile, American insistence on freedom of trade put increasing strain on relations with Germany. Britain, as master of the seas, was the chief beneficiary of commerce; Germany responded with

submarine warfare, inevitably sinking U.S. shipping. The issue
was not resolved. In 1917, Germany removed it altogether by an-
nouncing unrestricted submarine warfare on the assumption that
the United States would not, in case of war, be able to mobilize
quickly enough to be a factor. This was a bad error. The United
States went to war, mobilized, and its forces eventually tipped the
scales. The decision to enter was facilitated by the liberal February Revolution in Russia which toppled the tsarist regime and
thus made way (in the American view) for a "democratic" front
against autocratic, imperial Germany and Austria-Hungary. What
had looked like the usual European slaughterhouse in 1914 had
gradually stood forth, in Wilson's view, as a battle for democracy
as well as for a completely new kind of international relations, to
be based on collective security instead of balance-of-power politics.

Wilson was of course quite justified in indicting the system that
had produced, or at least allowed, the most egregious display of
butchery in history. A very nasty surprise, however, would soon
give his project a great deal more urgency: the advent of Bolshevism in Russia, October 1917. For not only did Lenin's regime take
Russia out of the war, it set forth a rigorously revolutionary critique of, and threat to, the system Wilson wanted to reform. Collective security, henceforth, was to be the antidote both to "the
irresponsible politics of the old world" and to Bolshevism, its monstrous stepchild. The new system would thus replace secret diplomacy with open agreements; feature self-determination as
opposed to territorial wheeling and dealing; guarantee the independent status of small states; open up the world economically
and dismantle exclusive spheres of influence; function on a basis
of moral norms and the common interest in agreement; and confront potential transgressors with concerted power. And on that
note the war ended on November 11, 1918, Germany capitulating
in the belief that the peace would follow Wilsonian precepts.

But the ensuing Treaty of Versailles of 1919 deviated in many
ways from these principles; it suffered, indeed, from being neither
crushingly punitive nor Wilsonian. It did, however, include as its
centerpiece his proposal for a League of Nations. He had pitched
it, not accidentally, as a "covenant." It was to be, in his words, "a

combination of the world for arbitration and discussion," a "wholesale moral clearinghouse." Since the criterion of self-governing rationality would determine who was to be allowed membership, Russia obviously did not qualify; and Germany would be on "probation." It was a universalist organization that was not universal.

In the fall of 1919, Wilson launched an epic campaign across the United States to get the treaty ratified. He was appealing not to the Senate but the public and thus wanted to invest his international reform with a specifically American meaning. So he resorted to the format, by now familiar, of a Protestant exhortation to fulfill the obligations that divine destiny so plainly had put before the American nation:

> The isolation of the United States is at an end, not because we chose to go into the politics of the world, but because, by the sheer genius of this people and the growth of our power, we have become a determining factor in the history of mankind. And after you have become a determining factor you cannot remain isolated, whether you want to or not. Isolation ended by the processes of history, not by the processes of our independent choice, and the processes of history merely fulfilled the prediction of the men who founded our republic.

Yet, as always, there was in fact a choice, the negative choice of turning away from one's obligation to "spiritual leadership" and denying that one had become "a determining factor" in world history. The United States was special, Wilson asserted, because it had "seen visions that other nations have not seen." Thus, prophetically, it had always been "destined to set a responsible example to all the world of what free Government is and can do for the maintenance of right standards, both national and international." Its mission, then, was "to be the mediator of peace," to be "the light of the world," and "to lead the world in the assertion of the rights of peoples and the rights of free nations." (And since Wilson imagined himself the embodiment of America, all this was really a mirror image of how he saw his own personal role in history.)

Turning away from one's deeper mission, in short, was to leave the rudderless masses of the world to their disorderly and darkish fate in the wake of the frightful war, when in fact they were yearning for American direction. The stakes were high, "the whole freedom of the world" and "the moral force of right" depending on "the choice of America." The moment for redemption, then, was at hand, for the nation was "in the presence of the realization of the destiny which we have awaited," its "manifest destiny." It stands to reason that choosing apostasy at such a critical juncture would not go unpunished. There would then come a moment when,

> in the vengeful Providence of God, another struggle in which, not a few hundred thousand fine men from America will have to die, but as many millions as are necessary to accomplish the final freedom of the peoples of the world.

By deliberately focusing on apocalyptic language and narrative form, I have distorted by omission the actual content of Wilson's message, which contained much pertinent and often persuasive argument about the workings of the treaty and the League. This should be remembered. What I want to show, however, is the importance of his millenarian commitment to the prophetic role of the United States. Unlike other nations, as he asserted, America "marches with its eyes not only forward but with its eyes lifted to the distances of history, to the great events which are slowly culminating, in the Providence of God, in the lifting of civilization to new levels and new achievements."

Beyond his attachment to the mission of "America," what of his new world order of reason? It deserves a comment or two. First, an antihistoricist notion of universal right such as Wilson's eliminates the geopolitical or spatial component of international politics: what is true is true everywhere at any given time. Interest and policy orientation have nothing to do, in theory, with history or geographical configuration. In this, Wilson differed radically from Roosevelt, who was extremely sensitive to spatial policy "flows," especially naval ones, and, sometimes, to the "situatedness" of norms as well.

More important, however, an order or organization supposed to embody the absolute principles of Right, the universal interests of humankind, tends to render any opposition to it inhuman or criminal. Wars to eradicate deviance from Right dehumanize the enemy. It is partly against this background that one must see the extraordinary fury of domestic repression, public and private, legal and extralegal, that took place in the United States once the country had entered the war: loyalty programs, savagery against "hyphenated" Americans and perceived dissenters from the American way of life, even lynchings. Radical movements were destroyed. Criticism of the war became illegal, and numerous people were imprisoned. Neither the experience of the Second World War nor even of the McCarthyist 1950s compares to the repression of domestic dissent during World War I. Wilson himself sensed no contradiction here in his odes to democracy and the popular voice, just as he saw no contradiction in arguing for public diplomacy while conducting it completely by himself, and just as he saw no contradiction in denouncing "imperialism" and intervention in the affairs of other nations while sending armies into Mexico and revolutionary Russia.

(3)

In 1899, Henry Cabot Lodge led the fight in the Senate to get McKinley's peace treaty with Spain ratified. A mere third of the Senate, he warned, should not be allowed to "repudiate the President and his action before the whole world." On a matter of such importance, it would be tantamount to "the humiliation of the United States in the eyes of mankind" and mark the American people as "incapable of great affairs, or of taking rank where we belong, as one of the greatest of the great world-powers." This, of course, was long before he became Woodrow Wilson's nemesis by leading the fight in the Senate against ratification of the peace treaty of 1919 and so of American entry into the League of Nations.

And thus the United States as a "determining force in history" retreated from the center stage of world politics, leaving the League to its sorry fate. Wilson's new world order, essentially, had been a nineteenth-century liberal attempt to implant in international relations a normative structure and a machinery for peaceful resolution of conflict, or at least the beginnings of such a system. It was hampered, therefore, by the same contradiction as liberal political theory in general: it assumed that if one channeled conflict between interests into a reasonable domain of norms and laws on the one hand, and allowed the autonomous processes of economic rationality free play on the other, then politics in the sense of antagonistic conflict would disappear. The political theory of liberalism is in that sense a theory of *depoliticization*, which is why it always ends up using illiberal, political means or criminalization when the irreconcilable returns.

Eminently liberal and American though it was (as he quite rightly emphasized), Wilson's formidable attempt to liberalize the world order was thus rejected by his own country, the most liberal power. What ensued was an abdication from geopolitical responsiblity coupled with inverse expansion of the economic and cultural presence of the United States in the world. The isolationist "normalcy" of the Republican 1920s was in that sense neither that isolationist nor that normal. Calvin Coolidge, nevertheless, expressed the spirit of his age by noting that Americans "have been, and propose to be, more and more American," by which he meant more and more businesslike. The essence of American "destiny," insofar as there was one, could only lie here. His successor, Herbert Hoover, a man of great internationalist credentials, concretized Coolidge's dictum by pointing out that, far from being destined for imperialism, Americans were busily constructing "a new economic system, a new social system, a new political system." In a different language, revolutionary new forms of capital accumulation were being invented, but the direction was inward. The United States would be an example to be emulated, not a Wilsonian regenerator.

It was Hoover's singular misfortune, however, to have to preside over the greatest single economic collapse ever suffered by the United States. Not even the ensuing New Deal could turn the exemplary nation into much of an example. Indeed, it would take a Japanese attack on the excellent harbor in Hawaii that God, as we have seen, had so obviously made for the American purpose of Pacific expansion to bring the United States finally out of the Depression and also irrevocably into the world. Was this the Fall, the corruption of the United States by a corrupted world, or the beginning of the final redemption of that world? The destinarian question of entanglement and separation would remain unresolved.

(4)

It is doubtful if Franklin Delano Roosevelt had any real hopes of redeeming Wilson's pledge to the "final freedom of the peoples of the world," but he certainly thought a beginning had to be made. Roosevelt followed the career of his distant relative Theodore to an almost comical degree, though he did so as a Democrat, starting out under Wilson to boot. Intellectually, he did not compare to these two figures of influence; but his political talent was peerless. His basic ideas about the postwar world and the American role in it are not easily discerned: Roosevelt was the most voluble yet enigmatic of American presidents. Like almost all of them he spoke of "destiny," but I doubt he thought twice about its deeper meaning. At his best he combined, not always logically, a deeply rooted Wilsonian disposition with Theodore's geopolitical nuance. Thus his new version of Wilson's League (that *would* have to be redeemed) included Theodore's idea of a concert of Great Powers exerting peaceful influence and vigilantly supervising their respective regions. The massive anti-Fascist alliance of the Second World War would be transformed, when the criminal aggressors had been vanquished, into a stable order of cooperation and mutual interest, headed by the United States, Britain, and the Soviet Union, perhaps also a reconstituted China.

This did not come to pass. In victory, Britain collapsed. China, a Great Power in theory only, became embroiled in civil war and revolution. The remaining two—gigantic continental powers, one heavily damaged, the other actually revitalized by the war— moved by default onto center stage, equipped with very little experience in taking charge of Great Power politics. Fundamental divergencies of ideology and socioeconomic system came to the fore. Within two years after Roosevelt had died and the war

ended, a wholly different and unintended kind of order, or an-
tiorder, had replaced the wartime alliance: the cold war. Henceforth, the United States would come to style itself as "leader of
the free world," locked in mortal struggle with the forces of Communist evil. This act of positioning harped back, not unnaturally,
to earlier themes of election and preordained mission. Once again
American destiny seemed manifest. In my final remarks I shall
sketch that cold-war projection of the United States in the world
until the moment when its contours begin to fade and the mission
loses meaning.

Convention has it that the cold war was identical with the entire postwar epoch up to the disintegration of the Soviet empire
around 1990. The origins of this equation are readily understand-
able. It was felt, quite rightly, that the U.S.-U.S.S.R. relationship
dominated international politics during the period. As that system
then dissolved, the nearest available catchphrase was eagerly
seized upon and thus "the end of the cold war" became an instant
cliché. Yet, as some may remember, Richard Nixon announced
the end of the cold war on his visit to Moscow in 1972, and so,
similarly, had others before him. Indeed, the Nixon-Brezhnev policy of détente fits ill with the connotations of a cold war. If in
fact that term is to mean anything it is surely to designate an
antagonistic conflict typical of war but without actual, open hostilities: an armed truce of "neither peace nor war." How did this
come about?

Negotiations between the victors about the postwar arrange-
ments in Europe faltered almost immediately and finally broke
down at the end of 1947. Subsequently, both sides moved to secure what they already controlled, the United States through the
introduction of the Marshall Plan and NATO, the Soviet Union
through the imposition of its own much more rigid and repressive
system throughout Eastern Europe. Mutual demonology ensued,
for both powers promulgated, and considered themselves to
embody, universal ideologies of right. This added intensity and
scope to the conflict, coding it in terms of capitalism versus
Communism, or, in the preferred Western war, freedom versus
totalitarianism. Diplomatic dialogue, normal relations, probing negotiation, and resolution of issues of mutual interest pretty much
ceased. This is what made the cold war a cold *war*.

Yet it did remain *cold.* Geopolitical and military realities served to keep the struggle preeminently in the realm of ideology. The rivalry generated an arms race of mind-boggling waste and destructiveness, and it fueled numerous deadly conflicts in the Third World; but never once did it escalate into open hostilities between NATO and the Warsaw Pact. By 1951, after the Korean War had developed into a stalemate, the line of demarcation between the two sides in fact became fairly stable, while the need to secure this territorialization amplified doctrinal purity on both sides of the fence. Launching savage attacks on the other, however, while pluming oneself in virtue, indicated no urgent desire to do anything actually unsettling. The two sides "found it convenient," if I may steal a phrase from Trollope, "to establish a mutual bond of inveterate hatred."

The American position was encapsulated in the concept of "containment," though it came to be far more militarized and global in scope than George F. Kennan, its originator, had had in mind. Like O'Sullivan, he was indeed initially unaware of having coined any such "historic" concept: others made it so. The assumption, in any event, was that the fanatical Soviet Union was inherently driven to world conquest, that the United States alone could contain it, and that once contained the Soviet Union would crumble, for, like all cancerous totalitarianisms, it needed to expand in order to survive. The actual result (if not the intention) of this analysis was a complete unwillingness to engage in any real diplomacy with the Soviet side, unless absolutely necesary. Diplomacy became a dirty word.

Though based on a fallacy, containment became an eminent success. The fallacy was the premise that the Soviet Union needed to expand. In fact, it probably needed the opposite, the relative isolation that actually followed, in order to survive as long as it did. But containment paved the way for the enormously powerful United States to expand its influence on a global scale and effectively establish hegemony over the world of industrial capitalism. This expansion was far more important than any relations with the eastern sphere. To push the American public into such an immense and unprecedented commitment, however, was no mean feat. Even though the United States after the war produced half of all manufactured goods in the world, it was still essentially an economy and a class structure anchored in domestic pursuits. The roots of the foreign-policy elite in the ruling classes overall remained shallow (and still do). Washington was in that regard a regime anomalously engaged in a global conflict but without firm footing in the domestic structure.

Eventually that footing would become materially more secure through the emergence of a military-industrial complex devoted to perpetual growth (and hence also to the idea of a perpetual threat). But at the outset it was necessary to simplify matters for Congress and the public. The Soviet Union was thus identified with Nazi expansionism by means of the category of totalitarianism. This deliberately scary vision culminated in a familiar exhortation *to choose righteousness in the face of historical fate*. A satanic force, dedicated to the overthrow of every sound and proven American principle, was abroad in the world, most frighteningly even at home through its fifth columns. To refrain from doing one's utmost to extinguish this evil was tantamount to sin and would end in self-destruction. The choice was plain. Only the United States could perform the given task. Would it rise to the occasion and do its appointed duty? And so forth.

I am abstracting a series of rhetorical moves here, not providing an inventory of arguments. Many other factors, geopolitical and economic, came into play. But the operative framework in which they all fit is the story of American exceptionalism, with its missionary implications. In no way could this task now be perceived as simply building something shining on the proverbial Puritan hill for the benefit of others to imitate; the moment for active regeneration had arrived. So the United States became "the leader of the free world," mobilizing and directing the forces of freedom against what Ronald Reagan would later call the Empire of Evil. That this Manichaean vision of good and evil in perpetual combat resonated among the public was not only because of the persuasiveness of the totalitarian story but also because of an underlying, new sense of vulnerability that had originated with Pearl Harbor. The atmosphere of fear thickened immeasurably when the Soviet Union detonated an atomic device in 1949 at the very same time as China "fell" to Communism. In reality, however, the United States remained largely impervious to devastation until the late 1950s.

The total, open-ended American effort recognized no shades of gray and no limits. Just as Protestantism had recognized no limits in the struggle against the satanic power of the Papacy, so the United States, occasional claims to the contrary, recognized none now except those of expediency. This was to be an epic struggle without restraint. Battle could, in principle, take place anyway, anywhere and anytime. And since the world was either white or black, every battle everywhere was by definition a victory for either one or the other. "If history has taught us anything," as Harry S. Truman opined, "it is that aggression anywhere is a threat to peace everywhere in the world." Every area was thus meaningful and important, every area worth fighting for.

It is instructive to compare this with earlier moments of expansion. In the 1840s, the spatial destination of destiny was clearly continental, a westward, horizontal movement; and the agent involved was the United States, separate and alone. In the 1890s the destination was diffusely conceived as a sphere of barbarism where the gradual struggle for civilization and race might occur on the way toward a final victory that was not that urgent; destiny was imagined more in historical than spatial terms; and the agent, though still the United States, was often seen in combination with other Anglophones, even the "West" in general. In the cold war, however, every space could in principle be defined with instantaneous and razor-sharp distinction either as our side or theirs, or as an arena not yet won where destiny would be fought out right now; and the United States was the global agent of freedom in lethal combat everywhere with a single, terrifying antagonist.

As critics pointed out at the time, there was a lack of discrimination in this last perspective. Everything was not in fact equally important, and gains for one were not necessarily losses for the other. That fact would eventually be revealed with great clarity in the punishing jungles of Vietnam. Vietnam would also destroy another part of the strategic map, the "domino theory." It held that if one area fell to Communism a succession of adjacent ones were bound to follow; so it could *not* be allowed to fall. Vietnam did indeed "fall" but without domino effect. Instead, Vietnam found itself at war with the People's Republic of China, its purported Communist master. The real lesson of the many lessons of Vietnam will then perhaps have been a greater suspicion of simple historical lessons.

Vietnam and the incendiary return of race through the civil rights movement combined to cause a legitimacy crisis in the United States comparable in depth only to that of the Civil War. The realities of Vietnam and the ghetto turned the messianic shibboleths of cold-war ideology into absurdities. Even something called the American Way of Life was put into question. Yet it is well to remember that a central theme of the critique was liberal, even destinarian: the "perversion" of true Americanism. Its radical potential had already been exhausted when the last American helicopter took off from the roof of the Saigon embassy in April 1975.

(5)

In 1963, just as the United States began to expand vastly the intervention in Vietnam, it established a more stable and manageable relationship with the Soviet adversary. The mutual interest that had always existed after the division of Europe had been reinforced by the emergence of nuclear arsenals capable of destroying either one or both in a matter of thirty minutes. The Cuban missile crisis in October 1962 illuminated this fact with frightening lucidity. MAD, "mutually assured destruction," expressed the new rationality in brilliant Pentagonese. It made sense, therefore, to tone down the irreconcilable differences of ideology and instead let the inherent Great Power logic of "conflictual cooperation" come to the fore, a development first symbolized in the Test Ban Treaty of 1963 and later reaching full force in the moment of détente. Fueling lethal conflict at a relatively safe distance in the Third World, and mostly at its expense, did not seriously threaten to undo this new geopolitical arrangement.

Great Power recognition made sense, then, within the world of geopolitics and the refined logic of nuclear balances, but it was never anchored very deeply in American politics. Managing global rivalry for mutual benefit continued to be a relatively autonomous activity, personified by the constantly airborne Henry Kissinger.

Thus the geopolitical shift corresponded to no basic change in the self-concept of the United States. And Kissinger aside, even the engineers of *Realpolitik* still imagined the United States as the specially anointed leader of something called the free world, though technically the crusade was to be replaced by intelligent management. There was, in short, a disjunction between geopolitical "realities" and the inward-looking orientation of American politics generally, producing an ideological gap of great potential difficulty for the maintenance of détente. One could ill afford extensive disturbances. By 1980, several such disturbances had occurred, most notably the Soviet invasion of Afghanistan.

The triumphant election of Ronald Reagan that year was a precise indication of how thin was the ideological acceptance of geopolitical realism and how wide was the receptivity to the themes I have discussed in this book. With great gusto and to much public acclaim, Reagan reasserted the true American Way in the world, using language strongly reminiscent of Jackson and O'Sullivan. His early jeremiads depicted a nation fallen temporarily on hard times because of atheism, welfare liberalism, government meddling, appeasement of Communism, and other deviations from the original and timeless faith. This catalogue of ills was always followed by the promise of regeneration, by a fervent evocation of the United States as a model fated to be revered, as one nation under God again, reaffirming the covenantal Constitution, specially blessed and once more believing in itself and the true American values. It was not an accident that Reagan launched his political career in 1964 with a speech entitled "A Time for Choosing"; nor that it ended with a rousing call for true courage in the "rendezvous with destiny." Indeed, he seemed to believe in a whole inventory of historical clichés: "that America was set apart in a special way, that it was put here between the oceans to be found by a certain kind of people," that it was chosen by higher authority to be "a beacon of hope to the rest of the world," that "the dream of America" was "the last best hope of man on earth." And so every American faced duties and obligations:

For with the privilege of living in this kindly, pleasant, greening land called America, this land of generous spirit and great ideals, there is also a destiny and a duty, a duty to preserve and hold in sacred trust mankind's age-old aspirations of peace and freedom and a better life for generations to come.

And this destiny and duty to the world meant above all vigorous prosecution of the cold war. Reagan came into the White House claiming expressly that he would not resurrect the cold war for the obvious reason that, as far as he was concerned, it had never ended. His intention, then, was merely to carry it out with proper determination and energy. He proceeded to act accordingly through a staggering military buildup and extremely chilly rhetoric. Even "Armageddon" made an apocalyptic appearance, if not prominently, in his vision of a showdown with the Soviet Union. Yet the very brevity of his attack on the "Evil Empire," the so-called Second Cold War, demonstrates nothing so much as the difficulties in reassembling the fundaments of the old system proper. As a way of using the federal budget for massive countercyclical spending to get out of a recession, his program made some sense (perversely, since he denounced the very idea of such a governmental role); similarly, it had meaning as part of his therapeutic move to restore popular confidence in the historical preeminence of the United States, the exceptional power second to none. Geopolitically, in the real as opposed to rhetorical world outside, the United States had little to win by it. And, typically, when the Soviet Union eventually responded by way of an ingenious policy of restraint and responsibility, Reagan swerved and became quite chummy.

He could then argue, and his epigones now do, that it was he who pushed the hated Soviet system over the edge by luring it into a race it could not keep up; and, therefore, that he triggered one of the greatest geopolitical advances in American history and fulfilled what was written in the stars. The Soviet demise, however, derived chiefly from long-standing domestic problems. Western consumer culture, if anything, had more to do with it than military hardware and virile belligerence.

The United States, meanwhile, has found itself without a central, defining adversary and so a bit lost, just as the Soviet Union initially had intended in the mid-1980s. Simple concepts superimposed on simple divisions and simple enemies no longer suffice as basic ideological props of American geopolitics. It is hard to imagine oneself "leader of the free world" when zones of gray are everywhere and there is no clear line between the free and the unfree. Deterritorialized capitalism, at the same time, is finally creating the world of fierce global competition without boundaries that Marx and nineteenth-century liberals alike once envisaged, thus deepening the disjunction between national politics and international economics. It is hard to talk of destiny when it seems to be determined by nothing so much as the impersonal logic of capital accumulation on a global scale. Meanwhile, Mahan was no doubt right. The purely utilitarian deity of the stock market does not mobilize people or confer political legitimacy on regimes, especially not at a moment when proliferating subidentities at home are making the meaning of "American" less and less obvious. Whither then the notion of mission and transcendence?

So I end by noting that never in U.S. history have prophetic destiny and mission been in such doubt. The instinctual return to Wilson is symptomatic of this. In the absence of simple enemies, his is the most identifiably American program available for those who wish the nation to play a cooperative yet leading role in the world. Law, ethics, discussion, "free enterprise" across borders, Western democracy: these are the key props of late-twentieth-century Wilsonianism, Americanism writ large in the name of humanity, as always hiding who really is involved and what really is at stake. Poised against it is another, more insidious form of prophetic Americanism. Inward-looking, it is the evocation of Jacksonian rapacity in the name of God and the "freedom" to exploit. The rhetoric is phantasmal and powerful, the political effect ferocious. Yet we are perhaps on the verge of some new and diffuse epoch where such projections will have limited moments in the sun because all that matters in the end is the perpetual present, a virtual reality empty of value, a postmodern world where destiny cannot be manifest and certainly not managed. When transcendence itself becomes nothing more than a commodity, the "sublime moral empire" of William Henry Channing's imagination must finally be dead. What will then be the fate, I wonder, of Melville's "Israel of our time," the "political Messiah" who would "bear the ark of the liberties of the world"?

BIBLIOGRAPHICAL NOTE

The imperative of brevity has made footnotes impossible. Instead, there is a series of bibliographical listings. They indicate some (only some) of the many intellectual debts I have incurred in writing this synthetic work. The selection is also designed to indicate a route to further study.

GENERAL

Albert K. Weinberg, *Manifest Destiny: A Study of Nationalist Expansionism in American History* (Gloucester, Mass., 1958 [1935]) remains the best study. Other useful works include Frederick Merk, *Manifest Destiny and Mission in American History: A Reinterpretation* (New York, 1966 [1963]); David M. Pletcher, "Manifest Destiny," in Alexander DeConde, ed., *Encyclopedia of American Foreign Policy* (New York, 1978); and Ernest Lee Tuveson, *Redeemer Nation: The Idea of America's Millennial Role* (Chicago, 1968). For documentary collections, see Norman A. Graebner, ed., *Manifest Destiny* (Indianapolis, 1968); Conrad Cherry, ed., *God's New Israel: Religious Interpretations of American Destiny* (Englewood Cliffs, N.J., 1971); and Allan O. Kownslar, *Manifest Destiny and Expansionism in the 1840's* (Boston, 1967).

On the "contextual" developments in the eighteenth and nineteenth centuries, see the two invaluable volumes by D. W. Meinig, *The Shaping of America: A Geographical Perspective on 500 Years of History*, vol. 1, *Atlantic America, 1492–1800* (New Haven, 1986); and *The Shaping of America: A Geographical Perspective on 500 Years of History*, vol. 2, *Continental America, 1800–1867* (New Haven, 1993). See also Michael Mann, *The Sources of Social*

Power, vol. 2, *The Rise of Classes and Nation-States, 1760-1914* (Cambridge, 1993); and idem, *States, War, Capitalism* (Oxford, 1988).

European Roots, Puritanism, Millenarianism, the Revolution

On Europe, see Robert Bartlett, *The Making of Europe: Conquest, Colonization and Cultural Change, 950-1350* (Princeton, 1993); Michael Mann, *The Sources of Social Power*, vol. 1, *From the Beginning to 1760* (Cambridge, 1986). David Hay, *Europe: The Emergence of an Idea* (Edinburgh, 1967), emphasizes the relative lateness of "Europe." As regards religious questions, see Ernest W. Nicholson, *God and His People: Covenant and Theology in the Old Testament* (Oxford, 1986); Dan Jacobson, *The Story of the Stories: The Chosen People and Its God* (New York, 1982); Norman Cohn, *Cosmos, Chaos and the World to Come: The Ancient Roots of Apocalyptic Faith* (New Haven, 1993); Adam B. Seligman, *Innerworldly Individualism: Charismatic Community and Its Institutionalization* (New Brunswick, 1994); Stephen D. O'Leary, *Arguing the Apocalypse: A Theory of Millennial Rhetoric* (Oxford, 1994); John J. Collins, *The Apocalyptic Imagination: An Introduction to the Jewish Matrix of Christianity* (New York: 1984); Christopher Rowland, *Radical Christianity: A Reading of Recovery* (Cambridge, 1988); Donald Harman Akenson, *God's Peoples: Covenant and Land in South Africa, Israel, and Ulster* (Montreal, 1991); Michael Walzer, *Exodus and Revolution* (New York, 1985); John F. Wilson, *Pulpit in Parliament: Puritanism during the English Civil Wars, 1640-1648* (Princeton, 1969); Brian Worden, "Providence and Politics in Cromwellian England," *Past and Present* 109 (November 1985): 55-98; Roger Crabtree, "The Idea of a Protestant Foreign Policy," in Ivan Roots, ed., *Cromwell: A Profile* (London, 1973); Christopher Hill, "Providence and Oliver Cromwell," ibid.; and idem, *Antichrist in the Seventeenth-Century England* (London, 1970). On prophecy and prognosis, see Reinhart Koselleck, *Futures Past: The Semantics of Historical Time* (Cambridge, Mass., 1985). On English destinarianism, J. C. D. Clark, *The Language of Liberty, 1660-1832* (Cambridge, 1994). Edmundo O'Gorman, *The Invention of America: An Inquiry into the Historical Nature of the New World and the Meaning of Its History* (Bloomington, Ind., 1961), is interesting on the differences with Spanish America.

On the discontinuity between England and New England, see Avihu Zakai, *Exile and Kingdom: History and Apocalypse in the Puritan Migration to America* (Cambridge, 1992). For a view stressing continuity, see David Cressy, *Coming Over: Migration and Communication between En-*

gland and New England in the Seventeenth Century (Cambridge, 1987).
On Puritan "symbology" I follow the seminal, if controversial, work of
Sacvan Bercovitch; see his *The Rites of Assent: Transformations in the
Symbolic Construction of America* (New York, 1993). See also Mason I.
Lowance Jr., *The Language of Canaan: Metaphor and Symbol in New
England from the Puritans to the Transcendentalists* (Cambridge, Mass.,
1980); James West Davidson, *The Logic of Millenarian Thought: Eigh-
teenth Century New England* (New Haven, 1977); and Charles M. Segal
and David C. Stineback, *Puritans, Indians, and Manifest Destiny* (New
York, 1977). For alternatives (some explicitly critical of Bercovitch), see
John Canup, *Out of the Wilderness: The Emergence of an American Iden-
tity in Colonial New England* (Middletown, Conn., 1990); Stephen Foster,
*The Long Argument: English Puritanism and the Shaping of New England
Culture, 1570-1700* (Chapel Hill, 1991); Philip F. Gura, *A Glimpse of Sion's
Glory: Puritan Radicalism in New England, 1620-1660* (Middletown,
Conn., 1984): Theodore Dwight Bozeman, *To Live Ancient Lives: The
Primitivist Dimension in Puritanism* (Chapel Hill, 1988); and Jon Butler,
Awash in a Sea of Faith: Christianizing the American People (Cambridge,
Mass., 1990). On the Revolutionary period, see Marc Egnal, *A Mighty
Empire: The Origins of the American Revolution* (Ithaca, N.Y., 1988); Mi-
chael Lienesch, *New Order of the Ages: Time, the Constitution, and the
Making of Modern American Political Thought* (Princeton, 1988); Nathan
O. Hatch, *The Sacred Cause of Liberty: Republican Thought and the Mil-
lennium in Revolutionary New England* (New Haven, 1977); and Robert
N. Bellah, *The Broken Covenant: American Civil Religion in Time of Trial*
(New York, 1975).

On empire and neoclassical arguments, see David Armitage's forth-
coming *The Ideological Origins of the British Empire* (Cambridge). See
also Dorothy Ross, "The Liberal Tradition Revisited and the Republican
Tradition Addressed," in J. Higham and P. Conkin, eds., *New Directions
in American Intellectual History* (Baltimore, 1979). The paradigmatic state-
ment of "neoclassical" historiography is J. G. A. Pocock, *The Machiavel-
lian Moment: Florentine Political Thought and the Atlantic Republican
Tradition* (Princeton, 1975). See too his "States, Republics, and Empires:
The American Founding in Early Modern Perspective," in Terence Ball
and J. G. A. Pocock, eds., *Conceptual Change and the Constitution*
(Lawrence, Kans., 1988).

On Thomas Jefferson, see the varied views in Joyce Appleby, *Without
Resolution: The Jeffersonian Tensions in American Nationalism* (Oxford,
1992); Garret Ward Sheldon, *The Political Philosophy of Thomas Jefferson*
(Baltimore, 1991); Robert W. Tucker and David C. Hendrickson, *Empire*

of Liberty: The Statecraft of Thomas Jefferson (New York, 1990); and Walter LaFeber, "Jefferson and an American Foreign Policy," in Peter S. Onuf, ed., *Jeffersonian Legacies* (Charlottesville, Va., 1993). On patriarchal theme, see Jürgen Gebhart, *Americanism: Revolutionary Order and Societal Self-interpretation in the American Republic* (Baton Rouge, La., 1993 [1976]); and Catherine L. Albanese, *Sons of the Fathers: The Civil Religion of the American Revolution* (Philadelphia, 1976). On relations with Britain, see Reginald C. Stuart, *United States Expansionism and British North America, 1775–1871* (Chapel Hill, 1988).

1820–1865

Aside from the primary printed sources mentioned in the text, I have used the following authorities and sources.

On O'Sullivan, see Julius W. Pratt, "John L. O'Sullivan and Manifest Destiny," *New York History* (14 July 1933): 213–34; and Sheldon Harris, "The Public Career of John Louis O'Sullivan," Ph.D. dissertation, Columbia University, 1958. My periodization of the antebellum period comes from Major L. Wilson, *Space, Time and Freedom: The Quest for Nationality and the Irrepressible Conflict, 1815–1861* (Westport, Conn., 1974). See also Arthur Alphonse Ekirch, *The Idea of Progress in America, 1815–1860* (New York, 1951); Fred Somkin, *Unquiet Eagle: Memory and Desire in the Idea of American Freedom, 1815–1860* (Ithaca, N.Y., 1967); Wilbur Zelinsky, *Nation into State: The Shifting Foundations of American Nationalism* (Chapel Hill, 1988); Anne Norton, *Alternative Americas: A Reading of Antebellum Political Culture* (Chicago, 1986). On race, see above all Reginald Horsman, *Race and Manifest Destiny: The Origins of Racial Anglo-Saxonism* (Cambridge, Mass., 1981). See too Michael Hunt, *Ideology and American Foreign Policy* (New Haven, 1987); and Ronald T. Takaki, *Iron Cages: Race and Culture in Nineteenth-Century America* (New York, 1979). On geographical "rationalism," see David N. Livingstone, *The Geographical Tradition* (Oxford, 1992). On art, see Albert Boime, *The Magisterial Gaze: Manifest Destiny and American Landscape Painting c. 1830–1865* (Washington, D.C., 1991).

On the 1840s, see Thomas R. Hietala, *Manifest Design: Anxious Aggrandizement in Late Jacksonian America* (Ithaca, N.Y., 1985); David M. Pletcher, *The Diplomacy of Annexation: Texas, Oregon, and the Mexican War* (Columbia, Mo., 1973); Norman A. Graebner, *Empire on the Pacific: A Study in American Continental Expansion* (New York, 1955); Bernard DeVoto, *The Year of Decision 1846* (Boston, 1942); Shomer S. Zwelling, *Expansion and Imperialism* (Chicago, 1970); Ramon Eduardo Ruiz, ed.,

The Mexican War: Was It Manifest Destiny? (New York, 1963); Gene M. Brack, *Mexico Views Manifest Destiny: 1821–1846* (Albuquerque, 1975); James M. McCaffrey, *Army of Manifest Destiny: The American Soldier in the Mexican War, 1846–1848* (New York, 1992); William R. Brock, *Conflict and Transformation: The United States, 1844–1877* (London, 1973); Paul F. Lambert, "The 'All-Mexico' Movement," in Odie B. Faulk and J. A. Stout Jr., eds., *The Mexican War: Changing Interpretations* (Chicago, 1973). For an interesting argument about expansion, see Loren Baritz, "The Idea of the West," *American Historical Review* 66 (April 1961). See also Patricia Nelson Limerick, *The Legacy of Conquest: The Unbroken Past of the American West* (New York, 1987). On the political map, see John H. Schroeder, *Mr. Polk's War: American Opposition and Dissent, 1846–1848* (Madison, 1973); Richard J. Cawardine, *Evangelicals and Politics in Antebellum America* (New Haven, 1993); Ernest McPherson Lander Jr., *Reluctant Imperialists: Calhoun, the South Carolinians, and the Mexican War* (Baton Rouge, 1980). On Fourierism, see Carl J. Guarneri's authoritative *The Utopian Alternative: Fourierism in Nineteenth-Century America* (Ithaca, N.Y., 1991). On intellectuals, Donald V. Gawronski, "Transcendentalism: An Ideological Basis for Manifest Destiny" (Ph.D. dissertation, St. Louis University, 1964), is an interesting, if overdrawn, account. On Melville, see Wai-chee Dimock, *Empire for Liberty: Melville and the Poetics of Individualism* (Princeton, 1989).

Among the works on or by various individuals used here are *The Diary of John Quincy Adams, 1794–1845*, ed. Allan Nevins (New York, 1951); *John Quincy Adams and American Continental Empire: Letters, Papers and Speeches*, ed. Walter LaFeber (Chicago, 1965); *Memoirs of John Quincy Adams, Comprising Portions of His Diary from 1795 to 1848*, ed. Charles Francis Adams, vol. 12 (Philadelphia, 1877); William Earl Weeks, "John Quincy Adams and Jackson's Seminoles," *Diplomatic History* 14 (Winter 1990); Leonard L. Richards, *The Life and Times of Congressman John Quincy Adams* (New York, 1986); Samuel Flagg Bemis, *John Quincy Adams and the Foundations of American Foreign Policy* (New York, 1949); Ernest N. Paolino, *The Foundations of the American Empire: William Henry Seward and U.S. Foreign Policy* (Ithaca, N.Y., 1973); *The Life of William H. Seward with Selections from His Works*, ed. George E. Baker (New York, 1860); Thomas Hart Benton, *Thirty Years' View*, vol. 2 (New York, 1968); Walt Whitman, *The Gathering of the Forces*, vol. 1 (New York, 1920); Sherry Penney, *Patrician in Politics: Daniel Dewey Barnard of New York* (Port Washington, N.Y., 1974); Theodore Parker, *Sins and Safeguards of Society* (Boston, n.d.); idem, *The Rights of Man in America* (Boston, 1854); George Bancroft, *Literary and Historical Miscellanies* (New York,

1857); Lilian Handlin, *George Bancroft: The Intellectual as a Democrat* (New York, 1984); Ralph Waldo Emerson, *Essays and Lectures* (New York, 1983).

Young America remains an understudied subject; but see Merle Curti, "Young America," *American Historical Review* 32 (October 1926). Filibusters have been well covered. See Joseph Allen Stout Jr., *The Liberators: Filibustering Expeditions into Mexico 1848–1862 and the Last Thrust of Manifest Destiny* (Los Angeles, 1973); Basil Rauch, *American Interest in Cuba: 1848–1855* (New York, 1948); Charles H. Brown, *Agents of Manifest Destiny: The Lives and Times of the Filibusters* (Chapel Hill, 1980); James T. Wall, *Manifest Destiny Denied: America's First Intervention in Nicaragua* (Washington, D.C., 1981); Anna Kasten Nelson, "Jane Storms Cazneau: Disciple of Manifest Destiny," *Prologue*, Spring 1986; Robert E. May, *The Southern Dream of a Caribbean Empire, 1854–1861* (Baton Rouge, 1973); idem, "Young American Males and Filibustering in the Age of Manifest Destiny: The United States Army as a Cultural Mirror," *Journal of American History*, December 1991.

1865–1914

Akira Iriye's *From Nationalism to Internationalism* (London, 1977) and Walter LaFeber's *The New Empire* (Ithaca, N.Y., 1967) are both excellent on foreign relations generally. On religion, see James H. Moorhead, *American Apocalypse: Yankee Protestants and the Civil War, 1860–1869* (New Haven, 1978); and Sydney E. Ahlstrom's classic *A Religious History of the American People* (New Haven, 1972). See also Kenneth M. Roemer, *The Obsolete Necessity: America in Utopian Writings, 1888–1900* (Kent, Ohio, 1976). On the state, I have followed Richard Franklin Bensel, *Yankee Leviathan: The Origins of Central State Authority in America, 1859–1877* (Cambridge, 1990); Stephen Skowronek, *Building a New American State: The Expansion of National Administrative Capacities, 1877–1920* (Cambridge, 1982). On imperial developments around the world, see Eric Hobsbawm, *The Age of Empire* (New York, 1987); and Michael Mann, *States, War, Capitalism* (Oxford, 1988). As regards expansionism in the 1890s, see Ernest R. May, *Imperial Democracy: The Emergence of America as a Great Power* (Chicago, 1991); Robert L. Beisner, *Twelve Against Empire: The Anti-Imperialists, 1898–1900* (New York, 1968); E. Berkeley Tompkins, *Anti-Imperialism in the United States: The Great Debate, 1890–1920* (Philadelphia, 1970); John Dobson, *Reticent Expansionism* (Pittsburgh, 1988); Jules R. Benjamin, *The United States and the Origins of the Cuban Revolution: An Empire of Liberty in an Age of National Liberation*

(Princeton, 1989); Julius W. Pratt, *The Expansionists of 1898: The Acqui-sition of Hawaii and the Spanish Islands* (Chicago, 1964 [1936]); Gerald F. Linderman, *The Mirror of War: American Society and the Spanish-American War* (Ann Arbor, Mich., 1974); David Healy, *Drive to Hegemony: The United States in the Caribbean, 1898–1917* (Madison, Wis., 1988); idem, *U.S. Expansionism: The Imperialist Urge in the 1890s* (Madison, Wis., 1970); Richard E. Welch Jr., *Response to Imperialism: The United States and the Philippine-American War, 1899–1902* (Chapel Hill, 1979); Walter L. Williams, "United States Indian Policy and the Debate of Philippine An-nexation: Implications for the Origins of American Imperialism," *Journal of American History* 66 (March 1980); Serge Ricard, ed., *An American Empire: Expansionist Cultures and Policies, 1881–1917* (Aix-en-Provence, 1990); R. Jeffrey Lustig, *Corporate Liberalism: The Origins of Modern American Political Theory, 1890–1920* (Berkeley, 1982); Emily Rosenberg, *Spreading the Eagle* (New York, 1982). Robert Dallek's essays in *The Amer-ican Style of Foreign Policy* (Oxford, 1983) are most useful. On Spencer and Darwinism, see Paul Crook, *Darwinism, War and History: The Debate over the Biology of War from the 'Origin of Species' to the First World War* (Cambridge, 1994); Greta Jones, *Social Darwinism and English Thought: The Interaction between Biological and Social Theory* (Brighton, 1980); Pe-ter J. Bowler, *Evolution: The History of an Idea* (Berkeley, 1984); Dorothy Ross, *The Origins of American Social Science* (Cambridge, 1991).

The following primary printed sources (and related works) proved of interest: Josiah Strong, *Our Country: Its Possible Future and Its Present Crisis* (Cambridge, Mass., 1963 [1891 ed.]); idem, *Expansion under New World Conditions* (New York; 1900); John Fiske, *American Political Ideas Viewed from the Standpoint of Universal History* (Boston, 1911); Milton Berman, *John Fiske: The Evolution of a Popularizer* (Cambridge, Mass., 1961); John W. Burgess, *Political Science and Comparative Constitutional Law*, vol. 1 (Boston, 1902 [1890]); Alfred T. Mahan, *The Interest of America in Sea Power, Present and Future* (Boston, 1918 [1897]); idem, *The Interest of America in International Conditions* (Boston, 1910); Owen Wister, *Owen Wister's West: Selected Articles* (Albuquerque, 1987); Henry Cabot Lodge, *The War with Spain* (New York, 1899); Carl Irving Meyerhuber Jr., "Henry Cabot Lodge, Massachusetts, and the New Manifest Destiny," Ph.D. dis-sertation, University of California at San Diego, 1972. Of the many works by Theodore Roosevelt, I used these: *The Man in the Arena* (Oyster Bay, N.Y., 1987); *Thomas Hart Benton* (New York, 1887); *African and European Addresses* (New York, 1910); *Selections from the Correspondence of Theo-dore Roosevelt and Henry Cabot Lodge, 1884–1918*, vol. 1 (New York, 1925); *Outlook Editorials* (New York, 1909); *The New Nationalism* (Englewood

Cliffs, N.J., 1961); *Fear God and Take Your Own Part* (New York, 1916); *Americanism and Preparedness: Speeches of Theodore Roosevelt, July to November 1916* (New York, 1917). Useful secondary works include Frank Ninkovich, "Theodore Roosevelt: Civilization as Ideology," *Diplomatic History* 10 (Summer 1986); David Burton, *Theodore Roosevelt: Confident Imperialist* (1968); Raymond Esthus, *Theodore Roosevelt and the International Rivalries* (New York, 1970). Robert I. Fulton and Thomas C. Trueblood, eds., *Patriotic Eloquence Relating to the Spanish-American War and Its Issues* (New York, 1900), is a very useful contemporary anthology of speeches. I also relied on the following journals: *North American Review*; *The Nation*; *The Forum*; *The Outlook*; *The Atlantic Monthly*; *Overland Monthly*; *Harper's Magazine*; *Review of Reviews*; and *The Literary Digest*. Contemporary books and pamphlets on the imperial moment include (New York, unless otherwise indicated): Theodore Marburg, *Expansion* (Baltimore, 1900); Charles Henry Butler, *The Voice of the Nation: The President Is Right* (1898); John White Chadwick, *The Present Distress: A Sermon upon Our Oriental War* (1899); John Henry Barrows, *The Christian Conquest of Asia: Studies and Personal Observations of Oriental Religions* (1899); John R. Mott, *Strategic Points in the World's Conquest* (1896?); George W. Crichfeld, *American Supremacy* (1908); John R. Dos Passos, *The Anglo-Saxon Century and the Unification of the English-Speaking People* (2nd ed., 1903); Goldwin Smith, *Commonwealth or Empire: A Bystander's View of the Question* (1902); Charles Gardiner, *Our Right to Acquire and Hold Foreign Territory* (1899); idem, *The Proposed Anglo-American Alliance* (1898); George S. Boutwell, *Problems Raised by the War* (Boston, 1898); Brooks Adams, *The New Empire* (London, 1903); idem, *America's Economic Supremacy* (1947 [1900]); Albert J. Beveridge, *The Meaning of the Times and Other Speeches* (1908); Walter Lippmann, *Early Writings* (1970); David Starr Jordan, *Imperial Democracy* (1901); James C. Fernald, *The Imperial Republic* (1898); Herbert Croly, *The Promise of American Life* (1964 [1909]); Randolph S. Bourne, *War and the Intellectuals: Essays by Randolph S. Bourne, 1915–1919* (1964); John Dewey, *The Middle Works, 1899–1924*, vol. 11 (Carbondale, Ill., various dates). Woodrow Wilson is best approached through *The Papers of Woodrow Wilson* (Princeton, various dates). The literature on him is immense. See, however, Niels Aage Thorsen, *The Political Thought of Woodrow Wilson* (Princeton, 1988); Lloyd Ambrosius, *Wilsonian Statecraft: Theory and Practice of Liberal Internationalism during World War I* (Wilmington, Del., 1991); and Thomas J. Knock, *To End All Wars: Woodrow Wilson and the Quest for a New World Order* (Oxford, 1992).

INDEX

abolitionism, 29, 39, 54, 59, 62

Adams, Brooks, 96

Adams, Charles Francis Jr., 103

Adams, John, 4–5

Adams, John Quincy, 18, 24–26, 31, 33, 34, 49, 59–61, 66, 105

Afghanistan, 42; Soviet invasion of, 127

Africa, colonization of, 72

agrarianism, 15–16, 22

agriculture, capitalist, 14, 22

Alaska, purchase of, 61, 62, 66

American Revolution, 4–5, 13, 19, 53, 55, 59; ideology of, 15, 16; monumentalization of, 20

American Whig Review, 39, 56–58

Anglicans, 4

Apaches, 38, 104

apocalypse, 9–10

Baja California, 37, 38

Bancroft, George, 52–54

Barnard, Daniel Dewey, 56, 58

Bellows, H. W., 57–58

Benton, Thomas Hart, 36

Berkeley, Bishop, 18, 66

Beveridge, Albert J., 97–100

Bible, 8, 59; Exodus, 4–7, 13; Genesis, 25; Revelation, 9, 13

Bismarck, Otto von, 73

blacks, 89–91, 102; citizenship granted to, 69; *see also* slavery

Blaine, James, 73

Boer War, 82

Bolshevism, 113, 116

Bonaparte, Napoleon, 53, 110

Boone and Crockett Club, 86

Boxer Rebellion, 75

Brezhnev, Leonid, 122

Brezhnev Doctrine, 108

Britain, 3, 17, 33–34; and annexation of Oregon, 35–36; in Boer War, 82; China and, 61; imperialism of, 72–74; India and, 42, 90; Mahan on, 84–85; in Napoleonic Wars, 23; navy of, 21, 71; republican ideology in, 15; in World War II, 121

Brockaway, Thomas, 19

Brook Farm, 51, 52